Praise for *Dreaming at the Gates*

"Intriguing! *Dreaming at the Gates* gently leads the reader into the mystery and adventure of deciphering our dreams and benefitting from their wisdom. Using the examples of actual dreams to unravel the messages, we learn how we can open to seeing beyond the facts to receive the guidance dreams can bring into our lives."

— KANI COMSTOCK, author of *Journey into Love: Ten Steps to Wholeness* and *Honoring Missed Motherhood: Loss, Choice, and Creativity*

"Kathryn Ridall, PhD, gives dreamers a beautiful book to help them deepen, understand, and call forth the creative forces that are alive in the multidimensional dream world within them. Woven through the personal sharing of dreams and stories, Dr. Ridall presents a history of using dreams in a healing capacity along with exploration exercises that offer guidance on how to work with dreams. She brings the wisdom of her years of personal and professional dream study to life in this rich guide to discovering the meaningful path of dreamwork."

— CHERYL KRAUTER, LMFT, author of *Surviving the Storm: A Workbook for Telling Your Cancer Story* and *Psychosocial Care of Cancer Survivors: A Clinician's Guide and Workbook for Providing Wholehearted Care*

"'Tell me what my dream means.' No can do. Only you, the dreamer, can crack the shell of your dream and be nourished by the meat inside. That's why this book is a terrific resource for you. Kathryn Ridall presents a Costco of dream theories and strategies to lead you to your style of nut. From classic theories to a famous author/psychic, reading each chapter is like trying out goodies from the Saturday demonstration stands at Costco. You are sure to find the right taste for yourself."

—Kathleen Sullivan, author of *Recurring Dreams: A Journey to Wholeness* and *Recurring Dream Symbols: A Map to Healing the Past*

"At different points in my life, I have been guided by the power of both ancestral and precognitive dreams. Thus, it was with great anticipation that I awaited this new work, *Dreaming at the Gates.* As readers of her work know, we always look to Kathryn Ridall to expand and deepen the conversation about the inner world, bridging scholarship with the intuitive process. This new book delivers it all. A psychotherapist and poet, Ridall draws us into her dreamscape and the dreams of others without dogma or device. Instead, she illumines a path by which each of us can find our own meaning in the world of dreams."

—Leslie Korn, author of *The Good Mood Kitchen* and *Natural Woman: Herbal Remedies for Radiant Health at Every Age and Stage of Life*

Dreaming *at the* Gates

Dreaming *at the* Gates

How Dreams Guide Us

Kathryn Ridall, PhD

DreamGate Press
Ventura, California

DreamGate Press
Ventura, California

Cover and interior design by Tabitha Lahr

Thanks to Coleman Barks, Daniel Ladinsky, Prartho Sereno, and the New Awareness Network Inc. for permission to include poems or parts of poems from their published works.

Printed in the United States of America

Print ISBN: 978-1-7331373-0-0
Digital ISBN: 978-1-7331373-1-7
Library of Congress Control Number: 2019912131

To the dreamer who lives within each of us.

Contents

Introduction

When I was in college, two friends and I formed a dream group that met weekly for a couple of years. We were young and knew nothing about how to work with dreams. Our ignorance was balanced by youthful enthusiasm and a deep-seated faith that our dreams meant something. We believed that if we unraveled the perplexing images of the dream world, we would find guidance for our lives.

Since those long-ago days, my devotion to dreams has remained steady. On most mornings I sit in an overstuffed chair in the morning light, a cup of tea by my side, a cat and a journal balanced on my lap. I record my dreams and my associations to the images, actions, and feelings of those dreams. With patient attention, the dreams begin to reveal their meaning.

Having followed my own dreams as well as those of my psychotherapy clients, I have a deep belief in the power of our dreams. Our dreams offer us reflections on the small day-to-day happenings of life, revealing imbalances or shortcomings in our conscious attitude. They also present powerful, transforming images that catapult us into new phases of life.

Most importantly, dreams release us from the predictable and often limiting perspectives of our waking selves. I consider it a great gift that amidst the challenges of life, we receive guidance and support from a different part of the psyche. Our dreams are not always easy. They can be challenging and downright terrifying. However, even the frightening ones bring our attention to issues we need to address. An alternative perspective and source of wisdom offers companionship and solace throughout all the stages of our life journey.

Dreams Calling

It's fitting and not surprising that dreams suggested this book to me before I had the conscious intention of writing a book. In the summer of 2017, my husband and I had been living in Ventura, California, for just over three years. I loved my beach town with its mild climate and its easy access to the sea, but I was at loose ends. Although I had a couple of new friends and a new psychotherapy practice in town, I was restless and dispirited. Something essential was missing from my life.

In August, I dreamed every night about searching for something—a new home, a new cat, a new church. As per my custom of titling my dreams, I called this first one "Looking for a Book to Write:"

> *I'm at a Christian gathering, A woman tells of an experience where she received a revelation from God about her destiny. That experience resulted in the church she now runs in her home. Her story is inspiring and I think, "I could collect similar stories and write a book about this kind of revelation."*

Two nights later, I had a dream I titled "Searching for My Guild."

I'm living in Fairfax, a small town in Northern California. I hear that there is a guild system in town. I'm trying to find the central office so I can see what guild I am assigned to. I think that it might be the writer's guild.

Both of these dreams pointed me toward a writing project. Although I wasn't likely to write an explicitly Christian book, I've always viewed life as a spiritual journey and have been interested in guidance that comes to us from beyond our waking selves. As I reflected on a specific topic, dreaming came to mind. As already noted, I've been moved and inspired by my own dreams and by those of my clients for many years. Writing a book about how dreams lead us forward on our path seemed like a meaningful way to honor the importance of dreams in both my personal and professional lives.

The Approach

From the beginning of this project, I knew that I wanted to collect dream stories that demonstrate how dreams work their magic in our life. Many books present a snippet of a dream to support a theory. I was drawn to telling dream stories in a bit more detail—what was going on in the dreamer's life at the time and how the dream impacted the dreamer's life.

To write this book, I gathered dream stories from a number of sources. I combed through my own dream journals and took an inventory of the most important dreams of my life. I re-read some of the writings of Swiss psychiatrist Carl Jung and American medium Jane Roberts, both courageous explorers of the dream world. I paid particular attention to how their own dreams influenced their understanding of the dream world. I also received permission from a few of my psychotherapy clients to include their dreams. Finally, I sent out a call for dreams to friends and colleagues, requesting a write-up of an important dream. In the course of time, many strangers also contributed their dreams.

After I received the write-up of a dream, I recorded an interview with the dreamer, either in person or on the phone. We talked in depth about the imagery and messages of the dream, and about how the dream affected his or her life. These interviews were inspiring. The contributors were surprised by the new insights that emerged as we talked. Both the dreamers and I were moved by the rich, unpredictable imagery in their dreams and by their dreams' powerful impact.

The Contributors

The contributors to this book are from many walks of life. They were raised and currently live in different parts of the United States. Each has had a lifelong interest in his or her inner life. Given their focus on the inner world, they are strong dreamers who report many years of vivid dreaming.

As I write these words, I'm aware that while everyone dreams, many people don't pay as much attention to their inner lives as do the contributors to this book. Life is often challenging and it can take all of our energy to make it through our days. Some people have a couple of important dreams, but don't have the bandwidth to track their dreams over time. However, just as a fine athletic performance or a powerful work of art inspires us by showcasing our human potential, so the reports of devoted dreamers reveal an important aspect of our human potential. We may not choose to follow our dreams, but we are all dreamers. The images and wisdom of the dream world are part of our human inheritance.

The Lay of the Land

This book is divided into twelve chapters. Each chapter explores dreams and how they affected the lives of the individuals who dreamed them. "Explorations," a short section at the end of each chapter, offers readers suggestions for working with their own dreams.

Chapter One
Into the Mystery explores the question of where our dreams come from and the cross-cultural belief that dreams are a source of wisdom and guidance. Tools for exploring dreams are presented.

Chapter Two
Carl Jung Confronts the Unconscious looks at Carl Jung's personal journey and some of the important dreams of his life. A brief introduction to his map of the psyche and the place of dreams in our development is presented.

Chapter Three
Jane Roberts and the Multidimensional Soul presents the life of Jane Roberts, and an introduction to the teachings of Seth, the intelligence she channeled. Roberts's explorations of the dream world to corroborate Seth's teachings are described.

Chapter Four
Early Illuminations delves into important childhood dreams that are remembered by adults. These remembered dreams are often harbingers of the dreamer's character and of themes that will preoccupy the dreamer's life.

Chapter Five
The Big Ones That Change Us looks at the "big dreams" that catapult us into a new phase in our inner or outer life. These

dreams can be inspirational, frightening, or both. They are often filled with archetypal imagery.

Chapter Six
Stepping Stones explores series of dreams that accompany us, step by step, dream by dream, during a particular transition or life passage.

Chapter Seven
The Ones That Come Again and Again looks at recurring dreams and their insistence that we pay attention to something. These dreams can feel relentless but offer comfort—our unconscious never gives up on us, even when we're slow to resolve an issue.

Chapter Eight
Nightmare and Solace investigates the dreams that comfort us and those that frighten us. Though we may prefer our dreams of solace, both kinds of dreams are important to our development.

Chapter Nine
Healing in the Dream World presents dreams that offer diagnosis and healing of physical ailments. These dreams can be precognitive, letting us know of a problem before it has been diagnosed.

Chapter Ten
The Final Gateway looks at dreams that help us come to terms with the death of our loved ones as well as with our own death.

Chapter Eleven
Visitations offers dreams in which we feel that we have been visited by otherworldly beings—the dead or beings that don't live

in this world. These dreams broaden our view of reality and can inspire creative and spiritual endeavors.

Chapter Twelve
Sharing Our Dreams presents ways that we can share the seemingly private experience of dreaming with others. Reporting our dreams to the people we live with and joining a dream group, in person or online, are ways to connect our dream world to others. Different kind of group dreamwork are explored.

Pure Gold

Early on in this project, the image of a beautiful golden bowl arose spontaneously in my mind's eye as a guiding image. The bowl was both radiant and empty. This image encouraged me to be receptive and to trust that this book would attract the support it needed. This was indeed the case. Over time, I received a steady stream of dreams, many of which took my breath away. I found editors and book crafters with wonderful skills. Friends and family offered various kinds of support, and finally, many people made financial contributions to the project.

Now, at the end of this project, I'm struck by another meaning of the golden bowl. It is an apt symbol for openness to our dreams and for the inner riches that come when we approach our dreams with patience and humility. Writing this book connected me to the gold I have received during a lifetime of dreaming and with the gold experienced by many other people who have faithfully worked with their dreams.

As you, the reader, engage with the dream stories in this collection, you will hopefully experience their power and be inspired to look more deeply for the meaning in your own dreams. Our dreams meet us at the gates of change, leading us forward us with their insight and support.

Chapter One

Into the Mystery

Each night as we sleep, we enter into the dream world, a place of mystery and wonder. In this alternate reality, we experience complex dramatic scenarios, set in many times and locations, including places that don't seem to be on our Earth at all. We interact with the living and the dead, with people we love and with complete strangers. Our dream self can be man or woman, adult or child. In dreams, we have abilities we will never have in our waking life, including abilities like flying or breathing underwater that are beyond our human capability. Our dream self's freedom and flexibility are stunning and unthinkable to our waking self.

The existence of the world of dreams raises many questions. What is the significance of experiencing two such different realities each and every day of our life? Is the dream world an imaginal world created by our brain or is it a different dimension of reality where we travel as we sleep? And regardless of the ultimate nature of dreams, what is their purpose? Do they exist solely to complement and guide our waking selves, or are they experiences that an unknown part of us creates for reasons in addition to guidance?

We humans have been considering these questions from the beginning of time, and yet our speculations can only be made by our waking selves and thus our answers are always limited. All we can say with certainty is that we experience two very different worlds throughout our lifetime, and in that sense, each of us experiences different dimensions of reality and is capable of navigating those different realities. When I think of the mystery of our dreaming, I am reminded of the words of the poet William Stafford, "The darkness around us is deep."

Our Bodies and the Dream World

The difference between our waking and dreaming lives is not surprisingly reflected in physiological differences between our waking and dreaming states. Each night, we experience several sleep cycles, each approximately ninety minutes long. Most of our dreams take place in REM sleep, named after the Rapid Eye Movements that occur during this stage. Some researchers have speculated that our eyes shift rapidly from side to side as they follow the unfolding dramas in our dreams.

We begin our sleep cycle in a light sleep that transitions us from waking consciousness through three stages of increasingly deep stages of sleep. In Stage 2 sleep, our heart rates and breathing patterns slow. In Stages 3 and 4, our brains produce slower delta waves. Our deepest sleep occurs in Stage 4, where we exhibit rhythmic breathing and limited muscle activity. The fifth and final stage of the sleep cycle is REM sleep, where we experience most, but not all, of our dreams.

Many physical changes occur during REM sleep. Our heart rates, breathing patterns, and brain waves all speed up from the preceding deeper sleep stages, perhaps as our psyche responds to the activity in our dreams. The slow delta waves of Stage 3 and 4 now shift to a "waking sleep" combination of alpha, beta, and desynchronized waves. Another intriguing fact is that our muscles become paralyzed. During non-REM sleep, our muscles are typically quiescent but able to function. During REM sleep, our muscles are unable to respond physically to the activity in our dreams. If we are engaged in an in-dream battle, we are unable to hurt ourselves or to lash out at the person lying next to us in bed.

Altogether, we spend about 20–25% of our sleep cycle in REM sleep. During our first sleep cycles, our REM sleep may be only five to ten minutes long. Most of our first sleep cycles is spent in Stages 3 and 4, during which our bodies repair and regrow tissues, build bone and muscle, and strengthen our immune systems. Toward the end of the night, Stages 3 and 4 shorten, and our REM sleep lengthens. During our final sleep cycle, we may spend a full hour in REM sleep. It seems that our body first takes care of its physical maintenance, and when its restorative tasks are completed, we move more deeply into the dream world.[1]

The Guidance of Dreams

Although our dreams present an alternate reality governed by different laws of time and space, we humans have always been drawn to this other reality. Throughout our history, we have believed that our dreams can guide us in our waking life. We have viewed the dream world as a sacred dimension and have sought to decipher the meaning of its often-puzzling offerings.

In indigenous cultures, a shaman was a technician of the sacred whose spirit traveled in trance and in nighttime dreams to obtain healing information for his people. In ancient Greece, people journeyed to the temples of Asklepios where, under the guidance of temple priests, they cultivated or "incubated" their own dreams to obtain Asklepios's assistance with health and other life matters.

In our contemporary world, dreams are seen as "the royal road to the unconscious," and contemporary psychotherapists help their patients use their dreams to resolve trauma and to receive guidance for life's challenges. Sigmund Freud, with a personal psychological focus, explored how dreams disguise unacceptable sexual and aggressive impulses in metaphorical "manifest" content. Carl Jung, as we will see in the next chapter, acknowledged the personal contents of our dreams, but was more interested in the universal imagery and themes that appear in them.

As descendants of Freud and Jung, many modern dreamworkers believe that dreams emerge from the unconscious, a part of the psyche different from our waking selves. We attempt to understand the image-driven language of the unconscious by exploring our individual as well as the cross-cultural associations to dream imagery.

Occasionally the images in a dream have such intrinsic power that we don't need to associate to them. Just sitting with those images deepens and guides us. Long ago, I had a haunting dream about a sick seal trapped in the indoor pool where I swam several times a week. In my waking life, I had had some doubts about the cleanliness of that pool. My dream clearly reflected my concern about whether the pool was healthy. The dream also said something about the state of my psyche at the time. I was feeling trapped in shallow, unhealthy waters, cut off from the deeper currents of life. Although I was helping my clients to touch into their deeper selves, I wasn't feeling that connection myself.

The seal dream presented an image of my predicament that saddened me, and I responded quickly to the dream's message about my plight. I left that gym with its dubious pool and also began to search for more expansive and nurturing circumstances in my life. I began to study my own dreams more intensively and to take workshops with various dreamworkers.

This particular dream presented a snapshot without any surrounding dramatic action. Although the images in our dreams don't always present their power so unequivocally and so starkly, many of the images in our dreams do offer experiences complementary to our waking lives. For instance, experiencing our dream self as a soldier, courtesan, or playful child, can open a parts of our selves that hasve been closed off and can encourage us to engage with that part of our selves in waking life.

The Second Mystery of Dreams

As we have seen, the primary mystery surrounding our dreams is metaphysical. Although we know that we can benefit from our dreams, we ultimately don't know where they come from or what they are. The second level of mystery is the meaning of any particular dream. At first glance, our dreams are famously confusing. There are no verbal explanation of the images and symbols, the dramatic scenarios and puns. Sometimes our dreams present a coherent drama, but there's no Playbill explaining how or whether that drama relates to our waking life. Although a few of our dreams may present a clear image, like my seal dream, most dreams need to be patiently tended to reveal their meaning. Even Carl Jung, who spent his life working with dreams, expressed humility about the initial encounter with a dream:

> So difficult is it to understand a dream that for a long time I have made it a rule, when someone tells me a dream and asks for my opinion, to say first of all to myself; "I have no idea what this dream means." After that, I can begin to examine the dream.[2]

Tools for Engaging the Mystery

Understanding the mystery of any dream can seem daunting, but we can develop tools for engaging with that mystery. The tools that follow are the ones that I use to work with my dreams. These tools, gleaned from years of study, are ones commonly shared by modern dreamworkers. I don't use each tool every time I engage with a dream, but work on any dream will utilize at least a couple of these approaches.

Creating a dream journal or notebook.

The unconscious, like other parts of us, responds to attention and acknowledgment. When we care enough to create a special place for our dreams, we signal our psyches that our dreams are important to us, and we begin to remember our dreams more regularly. In addition, when we have our dreams in one place, we have a record of them and can observe the development of different themes over time.

Writing the dream down in as much detail as possible, using the present tense.

When we write down our dreams, we create a bridge between our waking selves and our unconscious. We bring the experience of the dream world into waking life. Like many dreamworkers, I write my dreams in the present tense. This creates vibrancy and aliveness, as if the dream were still happening.

Allowing time for associations to the major images of the dream to emerge, and recording those associations.

Dreamwork takes time. Setting aside time for our associations to emerge is essential. We are often surprised by the memories, hopes and aspirations, anxieties or worries that arise in response to a dream's images. Although we might not have predicted those associations, they reveal the layers of meaning embedded in a dream's imagery.

Identifying our feelings in the dream and after awakening.
One of the most powerful tools for understanding our dreams is our feelings both within the dream and upon awakening. Sometimes the feelings of the dream alone can orient us to its meaning. In those instances, we recognize the feelings of the dream as the very ones we're experiencing toward an issue in our life and we know that this dream is connected to that issue.

Often, however, it's a little more complicated. As we call up our associations to a dream image, we discover the feelings we have toward the images and our associations to the images. Maybe we dream about being a pirate. We feel exhilarated by being on the open sea and, upon awakening, we realize that it's been a long time since we've felt alive in that way. We realize that we feel overly domesticated and confined in a life that has become too safe and predictable. We're probably not going to become a pirate, but we may pick up our surf board or plan a backpacking trip.

Sometimes our feelings within the dream and upon awakening are different. For instance, we might feel frightened in our dream when our pirate self faces an enemy, but when we wake up we feel exhilarated by our courage and stamina. This discrepancy between the feelings of our dream self and waking self might alert us to something in life that is hard to do but that will increase our self-esteem and sense of aliveness.

Considering the location of the dream.
The location or our dreams tells us a good deal about the arena of the life our dream is addressing. If we're in our childhood

home, we might look first for early family issues that might be at play in the dream and that also may be activated in our current life. If we dream about the place we met our spouse, the dream may be addressing something in our marriage.

Understanding the experience and perspective of each of the major characters in the dream drama.
Our dreams are often dramatic events with several interacting characters. To understand the meaning of a play or a movie, it's essential to understand the motivation of each character. The same is true of understanding the drama in a dream. If there is a conflict, it's important to understand the perspective of each character. If the perspective of a character is unclear or seems particularly important, we might create a dialogue with that character and write that dialogue down in our dream journal.

Viewing each character as part of oneself.
Since some part of us creates all of the characters in a dream, each character can be seen as expressing part of the dreamer. When there is conflict between characters in our dream, that conflict might represent tension in our psyches and in our outer lives. Maybe our pirate dream -self has a wife who wants him to give up the sea and stay on land. This could reflect an internal war between routine and freedom, relatedness and adventure.

Tracking the arc of action in a dream.
Sometimes in spite of our best efforts, the meanings of a dream remain elusive. Our associations are meager and we don't know why we're dreaming about a pirate or our dead grandmother. However, when we look at the dramatic arc of action in the dream, such as loss or the inability to complete a task, we better understand the issue being addressed and how that relates to our life.

Giving the dream a title, and entering that information in an index at the back of the dream journal.
The title is a way of distilling the essence of a dream. An index is a useful way to recognize themes that might recur in a given period of time.

"Not Getting the Task Done"

About six months into writing this book, I had a dream which I titled "Not Getting the Task Done." How I worked with this dream might provide a clearer sense of how to apply the preceding tools.

> *I am an adult living in a house with a family that includes a sixteen-year-old girl. This teenager has a car which during the course of the dream is rammed repeatedly by a punk in a low-rider. The girl takes off and I, as the responsible adult, gather the miscreant's license and insurance card, and place them on a table next to the rammed car. This table is littered with piles of paper and debris, and I promptly lose both the license and the insurance card. I spent the rest of the dream in befuddled state, fumbling through the mass of papers, unable to find the documents.*

When I awoke from my dream, I felt befuddled and frustrated, just as I did in the dream. The first thing I looked at was the surface scenario of the dream. Did it resemble anything in my life? The answer to that question, as is so often true with dreams, was no. I don't live in a family that includes a sixteen-year-old, and I have never had my car rammed. Furthermore, I don't know anyone whose car has been rammed. Although the arc of action in the dream didn't mean much to me, I was able to recognize the emotional befuddlement of my dream self as similar to my current feelings about my dream book. After a strong start where I took responsibility and had clear intentions (confronting the driver and getting both his license and insurance card), I had fallen into doubt and was aimlessly sorting through papers.

Having identified a primary issue of the dream, I looked at the different characters. There was the sixteen-year-old who abdicated responsibility and ran away. When I asked if part of me was running away from the dream project, I had to admit how often I abandoned the project for weeks at a time. That inner teenager threw out thoughts like, "Wouldn't I rather walk at the beach or meet a friend for coffee? Why don't I write a poem instead? Why don't I spend my time doing something that's more fun?"

I then looked at the punk who rammed into the girl's car and made her car dysfunctional. I asked myself, "Is there a punk in me that is ramming into my car, undermining my ability to move out into the world with this project?" It wasn't difficult to identify the stream of negative thoughts that had been ramming into my confidence about the project: "I have nothing new to say about dreams, so why bother to put time and energy into writing a book? I'm going to spend months on this project and it's not going to mean anything to anyone but me."

Once understood, this dream painted a clear picture of warring parts of myself: the adult who was trying to carry out her tasks but had lost focus, the inner teenager that didn't want to take on the responsibility, and the punk who was undermining my confidence. The dream didn't tell me what to do, but it did paint a clear, if unflattering, picture of my stagnation with the dream project.

As with any dream, it was up to my waking self to decide how to work with the information the dream presented. My dream project was precious to me and so I decided to move forward with it while keeping close watch on my inner teenager and punk. I won't pretend that those sabotaging voices disappeared. Their attitudes appeared many times during the writing of this book. However, this dream helped me to recognize these attitudes and to move through them more quickly than I might have if I hadn't had the dream.

Valuing the Mystery of Our Dreams

As we work with our dreams and benefit from the guidance they offer, we learn to value the mystery that surrounds them. I may not know the ultimate metaphysical nature of "Not Getting the Job Done," but I do know that working with the imagery of that dream helped me to better understand my relationship to this book at that point in time. That dream helped me to move forward with this project. As we work with our dreams over time, we gain confidence in a consciousness that assists our waking selves and that guides us. We may not fully understand the origin or the nature of that consciousness, but we know it's there to help us.

Similarly, as we spend time with our dreams, we learn to value our initial confusion. Our lack of understanding is a predictable part of the process of working with a dream. The lack of verbal explanation, like the flexibility of our dream self, is verification of a dimension of experience very different from our waking life.

In this chapter, we have looked at some of the mysteries of the dream world. In the next chapters, we will look at the work of two geniuses of the dream world, Carl Jung and the American medium Jane Roberts. Each of them dove deeply into the unconscious, attempting to understand the reality our dreams emerge from and the contributions our dreams make to our development. Both of these dreamers took risks to explore the dream world. Both left art and extensive writing about what they learned from their journeys into the unconscious.

Explorations

- Delve into your own beliefs about what dreams are and what they offer. As you look back on your life, have you had important dreams? How did they affect your life?

- If you want to deepen your relationship with your dreams, it's important to start a dream journal. It doesn't matter if it's paper or electronic. The important thing is that you have easy access to it and that you feel comfortable using it.

- What kind of daily ritual can you set up to record and work with your dreams? On days when you're too busy to spend time, what kind of shorthand system can you create to remember the dream for later when you have the time to record and work with it?

- Do you have adequate tools to explore the meaning of your dreams? Look at the tools presented in this chapter to see which ones you're using and which are new to you.

- Pick out a dream that has affected you, but that has remained a mystery. Set aside some time to explore the dream using the tools in this chapter.

- Do you have friend or family member who would share dreams with you? Maybe there's a dream group or a workshop in your community or online. Sharing dreams makes the journey more fun and helps us develop our dreamworking skills.

Chapter Two

Carl Jung Confronts the Unconscious

Carl Jung was one of the great dreamers of the modern era. A record of his intensive engagement with his dreams is found in his autobiography, *Memories, Dreams, Reflections,* and also in *The Red Book*, which presents his midlife encounter with the unconscious in the style of an illuminated manuscript. Jung's understanding of dreams was gleaned from his own experience and those of his patients, as well as from his study of psychology, mythology, philosophy, and religion. Jung's lifelong call to explore the unconscious and dreams began at age three with a dream about a subterranean temple. This childhood dream launched his long engagement with dreams.

Carl Jung was a sensitive child, deeply affected by the images and emotions around him. Ongoing tension between his parents permeated his home and created insecurity in his early life. When he was two, his mother was hospitalized for several months and a maiden aunt cared for him. In his autobiography, Jung noted that this separation from his mother was deeply troubling and increased his sense of insecurity.

Jung's childhood was steeped in the imagery and practices of Christianity. His father was a pastor in the Swiss Reformed Church, and eight of his uncles were parsons. Some aspects of his Christian upbringing, like early morning prayers, were comforting to him. Other aspects were frightening. The image of the bloody corpse of Jesus was disturbing, as were funerals, where dark, gloomy pastors lowered bodies into the ground to rest in the arms of Jesus. The youthful Jung couldn't quite trust Jesus. As he later wrote, he secretly doubted Lord Jesus' loving kindness.[3]

When Jung was three, he had his dream about a subterranean temple. This dream presented imagery quite different from anything he had encountered in his waking life. In this early dream, he was in the meadow behind his house where he found a stone-lined opening with steps leading down into the earth. At the bottom of the stairs stood an archway closed off by a green brocade curtain. Opening the curtain, he found a chamber of stone with a red carpet leading through the center of the room. At the end of the room was a golden throne and on it, something surrounded by an aura of light:

> Something was standing on it which I thought at first was a tree trunk twelve to fifteen feet high and about one and a half to two feet thick. It was a huge thing, reaching almost to the ceiling. But it was of a curious composition: it was made of skin and naked flesh, and on top there was something like a rounded head with no face and no hair. On the very top of the head was a single eye, gazing motionlessly upward.[4]

Jung was both terrified and awestruck by this dream that provided a sacred image at odds with the Christian symbols surrounding him. He never forgot this dream, and throughout his childhood, whenever someone talked too passionately about the

Christian God, the image of this other god returned to his mind. This dream provided an alternative to the oppressive aspects of the Christian world around him. It also initiated an inner life of dreams and private rituals that may have counter-balanced some of the tensions in his family situation.

Although Jung's unhappiness in his personal circumstances may have fueled his early attraction to other realms, the image of the subterranean temple was transpersonal. It came from somewhere beyond his personal fund of imagery and knowledge. Only much later would Jung learn about the phallic symbolism found in the iconography of non-Christian religions.

This dream raised the question of how such a dream came to a small child in Switzerland. Jung later mused, "Who was it speaking in me? . . .What kind of superior intelligence was at work?"[5] This dream and other early experiences laid the base for Jung's lifelong investigation of the unconscious as an objective reality, filled with images and perspectives very different from those of the conscious mind.

Confrontation with the Unconscious

Jung's most intensive investigation of his unconscious and of his dreams extended for several years, beginning when he was in his late thirties. At this time, he was an established psychiatrist, a university professor, and a published author. He was also a husband, and a father of five children. Although Jung had achieved many of the outward markers of success, he entered an extended period of emotional upheaval that began after the rupture of his relationship with Sigmund Freud in 1912.

Freud, the genius often identified as the father of modern psychology, had accepted Jung as a kind of son and successor. The two men had been strongly drawn to each other, but there was disagreement between them from the beginning of their relationship. Freud believed that the dynamics in our psyches arise from the tension between our instinctual drives, particularly sexual, and the restrictions of civilized life. He viewed dream imagery as disguised wish-fulfillment growing out of this tension. Our dream imagery could also indicate a neurosis resulting from the repression of our instincts.

Jung, with his rich history of dreaming, felt that our psychodynamics are more than a struggle with repressed sexual urges. He believed Freud's views on dreams were reductive, and that our dreams are responsive to many types of life experiences. He also felt that Freud's views of dreams overlooked the mysterious richness of our dream imagery, like his own early dream of the subterranean temple. Dream imagery for Jung wasn't merely a disguise for sexual conflict. It was a natural, if often puzzling, language that says what it means. Our task is to decipher that language.[6]

When Jung broke with Freud, he knew he differed from Freud, but he had not yet formulated his theory of a shared collective unconscious. Jung almost certainly needed to break with Freud to follow the path of his own genius. However, he also had felt disoriented by the loss of that relationship. Many of his colleagues shunned him after the rupture, and he lost his position in the psychoanalytic world. In the years that followed, Jung's inner life was often overwhelming to him. He experienced upsurges of strong, unexplained emotions and extremely vivid dreams and visions. He called the process of these years his "confrontation with the unconscious."

In some sense, Jung had little control over this encounter with the unconscious, but from the beginning he experienced himself as an active collaborator. He was interested in observing the workings of his own inner life to better understand the human psyche. As he wrote in his autobiography, "From the beginning I had conceived my voluntary confrontation with the unconscious as a scientific experiment which I myself was conducting and in whose outcome I was vitally interested."[7]

During the years of this intense process, Jung often feared for his sanity. He practiced yoga to calm himself when he was buffeted by strong, inexplicable emotions. He sought to find the images and experiences underlying his tumultuous inner state. He followed his dreams closely, painting his important dream images and engaging in imaginal dialogues with dream and visionary figures. He collected his experiences in what he called "the black books." Later he copied and embellished these images in the style of an illuminated manuscript in a document he called *The Red Book.*

Jung's engagement with his inner life was also grounded and facilitated by his work with stone. He returned to a practice of his childhood and built a miniature town from stones. He carved stones that were symbols of his inner journey. His work with stone and painting both grounded him and encouraged his unconscious to produce more material.[8]

As noted, during these years, Jung feared that his inner life would overwhelm his ego and that he would descend into a psychosis. Several factors helped to prevent this. His relationship with his wife and five children, and the routines of family life, stabilized him and gave him grounding in the outer world. His work with his patients also tethered him. He believed that what he was learning would help them. This sense of purpose helped him to maintain his observing self and to create some helpful distance from his tumultuous inner life.

A final, crucial factor in both his survival and the development of his map of the psyche was his relationship with Toni Wolff, a brilliant analyst who was his personal companion and his collaborator. During these crucial years, the two of them worked closely together, tracking Jung's dreams and fantasies. Both of them believed that his confrontation with the unconscious was in service of mapping the human psyche. Their close connection kept Jung from slipping away into psychosis.[9]

The Death of Siegfried

The following dream occurred in the winter of 1913 during the early days of Jung's encounter with the unconscious. He was already committed to his inner exploration in service of the science of psychology. However, he also felt humiliated by his situation. Playing with stones and feeling overwhelmed by emotions and visions was humbling to the brilliant doctor who once had the psychoanalytic world at his feet. Jung's dream about Siegfried, the mythical German warrior, follows:

> I was with an unknown, brown-skinned man, a savage, in a lonely, rocky mountain landscape. It was before dawn, the eastern sky was already bright, and the stars fading, Then I heard Siegfried's horns sounding over the mountains and I knew that we had to kill him. We were armed with rifles and lay in wait for him on a narrow path over the rocks.
>
> Then Siegfried appeared high on the crest of the mountain, in the first ray of the rising sun. On a chariot made of the bones of the dead he drove at furious speed down the precipitous slope. When he turned the corner, we shot him dead.
>
> Filled with disgust and remorse for having destroyed something so great and beautiful, I turned to flee, impelled by the fear that the murder might be discovered. But a tremendous downfall of rain began, and I knew that it would wipe out all traces of the dead. I had escaped the danger of discovery; life could go on, but an unbearable feeling of guilt remained.[10]

The desperation of Jung's state at the time was indicated by an inner voice that spoke to him after this dream and counseled him that if he didn't make sense of this dream immediately, he would have to shoot himself. Since Jung had a loaded revolver close by, he had incentive to come to some understanding of the dream.

On reflection, Jung understood that Siegfried was like the Germans who were trying to impose their will on the early twentieth-century world order. However, he also recognized Siegfried in his ego's desire to be the hero and to dominate his inner and outer lives. Jung's dream self was accompanied by a savage, representing the hidden, unconscious parts of himself that were now emerging.

From this dream, Jung understood that the willful, heroic part of himself was no longer dominant and that he must engage with the unconscious parts of himself. This dream clearly reflected his humiliation that his ego could no longer dominate his destiny. As the dream indicated, Jung felt remorse, guilt, and sadness about losing his heroic self, but his dream clearly indicated that he would have to trust his own unconscious process.

This content of the dream and Jung's response to it are hallmarks of what would become staples of the Jungian approach:

- letting go of the conscious ego's domination;
- trusting that the imagery of our dreams and visions is meaningful; and
- deepening the engagement with our dreams and visions by painting their imagery and by dialoguing with dream and visionary figures.

The Arrival of Philemon

Jung's engagement with the unconscious during these seminal years included interacting with fantasy figures that came to him in dreams and visions. His imaginal dialogues with various fantasy figures yielded much unexpected learning. The most important of these inner figures was Philemon, who first came to him in a dream.

> There was a blue sky, like the sea, covered not by clouds but by flat brown clods of earth. It looked as if the clods were breaking apart and the blue water of the sea were becoming visible between them. But the water was the blue sky. Suddenly there appeared from the right a winged being sailing across the sky. I saw it was an old man with the horns of a bull. He held a bunch of four keys, one of which he clutched as if he were about to open a lock. He had the wings of the kingfisher with its characteristic colors.[11]

Jung initially didn't understand the significance of this figure. As was his custom, he painted it. While he was working on this painting, he found a dead kingfisher in his garden. He was "thunderstruck" by this occurrence, given that kingfishers were very rare in Zurich. This synchronicity provided a sense of greater connectedness and meaning to this dream encounter.

Soon after having this dream, Jung began to have conversations with Philemon in his imagination. In these dialogues, he received a good deal of information about the process he was in. Philemon became a guru or spiritual teacher to him.

Years later, when Jung had a conversation with a cultivated Indian man about the guru-disciple relationship, the man mentioned that his guru was Shankaracharya, who had died centuries ago. When Jung questioned whether he meant the spirit of Shankaracharya was his teacher, the man answered that this was so, that there are always some people who have a spirit for a teacher. Jung thought of Philemon and felt comforted that his own experience was a part of a greater collective experience.

Jung's relationship with Philemon was important because of the needed guidance that Philemon provided. It was also important because Philemon had perspectives distinct from Jung's. Philemon knew things that Jung did not. From his interaction with Philemon, the unconscious was further verified as an objective place filled with images, perspectives, and figures quite different from the dreamer's. As Jung wrote:

> Philemon and other figures of my fantasies brought home to me the crucial insight that there are things in the psyche which I do not produce, but which produce themselves and have their own life. Philemon represented a force which was not myself.[12]

Through many years of experiencing dreams like the one with Siegfried and imaginal relationships like that with Philemon, Jung developed his own map of the psyche, and a theory of how our psychic development occurs. A few of basic elements of Jung's theory, relevant to understanding the dreams in this book, follow.[13]

Jung's Map of the Psyche

The Ego

Jung's map of the psyche includes the *ego*—the conscious, waking part of the self that mediates between our inner impulses and the outer world. This part of the self helps us to survive in the outer world, to deal with our unruly impulses, and to realize our most cherished goals. The ego is the conscious part of the psyche that most of us identify with, although from Jung's perspective, the ego is a very small part of our psyche. For Jung, the vast majority of our psyche resides in the deeper, unknown levels of our unconscious.

The Personal Unconscious

Lying closest to our waking ego is the *personal unconscious*, filled with our repressed impulses, traumas, and the many experiences that we take in, but haven't yet consciously processed. Much modern-day psychotherapy helps us to integrate the experiences in our personal unconscious that are wreaking havoc in our emotional life. When we have material in our personal unconscious that needs to be integrated, we may have dreams and recurring dreams that bring that unconscious material to our attention.

The Collective Unconscious

The ego and the personal unconscious have been part of every psychodynamic model since Freud. Jung brought his own unique genius to bear in identifying a *collective unconscious.* As we have seen, beginning with his early dream of a subterranean temple, Jung experienced dream contents that didn't arise from the images in his waking life. As he developed his map of the psyche, he identified a collective layer of the psyche, with images and knowledge shared by people across cultures and time. Although the content of dreams, visions, and myths are influenced by culture, the *archetypes* or patterns for shaping experience are universal.

As an example, Jung's dream self in the Siegfried dream is a Germanic hero. A dreamer from another culture would have another hero to represent the hero in himself—Maui in Hawaii or Arjuna in India. Similarly, Jung experienced the archetype of the inner guru in Philemon. As mentioned, Jung once encountered an Indian man who talked about his guru-disciple relationship with the long-dead Shankaracharya. Both Jung and this Indian man were engaged with the archetype of the inner guru, but the form of that teacher was influenced by their respective cultural influences.

Individuation

An important part of Jung's understanding is that our psyche is always evolving, continually seeking greater wholeness. Each of us has a set of potentialities—some instinctual, some cultural, and some personal, like our unique talents and passions. Over a lifetime, our potentialities move from the unconscious to conscious expression in the outer world. Jung called this lifelong process, of realizing our potentialities and seeking greater wholeness, *individuation.* An ongoing dialogue between the conscious and unconscious parts of our personality is an essential aspect of our individuation.

The Self

For Jung, the process of individuation is far from random. There is an order to each person's unfolding that is influenced by the true center of his or her personality, the *self.* While the ego helps us to order the outer world, the self resides deep within the psyche and helps to coordinate all parts of our psychic lives. The self is the true center of evolving consciousness. When there is a strong connection or axis between the ego and the self, life unfolds with meaning and purpose.

Compensation

In Jung's thought, the mechanism that propels our ongoing individuation is *compensation.* The ego, with its controlling agendas of security and survival, tightly limits our waking perspectives and makes us one-sided. Our dreams help us to move beyond this one-sidedness by offering balancing perspectives. Sometimes our dreams originate from the material contained in our personal unconscious. Our big, life-changing dreams most often involve the activation of an archetype from the collective unconscious.

Jung wrote the following about compensation:

> The unconscious is the unknown at any given moment, so it is not surprising that dreams add to the conscious psychological situation of the moment all those aspects which are essential for a totally different point of view. It is evident that this function of dreams amounts to psychological adjustment, a compensation absolutely necessary for properly balanced action.[14]

Jung's Place in this Book

The understanding I bring to the dream stories in this book is indebted to Jung. When I discovered Jung's work forty years ago, it was like finding a longed-for older brother and guide. I have had many experiences similar to his, including a pivotal early dream followed by a lifetime of important dreams. I have also interacted with visionary figures who taught me as Jung was taught by Philemon. Since my early twenties, I have sensed the existence of a deeper self, separate from my ego, and have experienced an individuation process that is palpable to me, not an abstraction. In Jung, I found a fellow traveler and a teacher who articulated my own experience of the world.

Just as Jung's legacy has been pivotal to my own understanding, it has also been important to many, although not all, of the dreamers in this book. Many of the dreamers in this collection have felt guided by dreams throughout their lives and have a strong sense of a deeper, guiding self as well as of an individuation process at work in their lives. Some of these dreamers used Jungian terminology to describe their understanding. Others used different words for the same concepts. Some of the dreamers have encountered Jung's work directly. Others may have been, knowingly or unknowingly, exposed to his ideas through people and books influenced by him. Each of the dreamers has a different relationship to Jung, but the genius of this explorer, healer, and theoretician is alive and well in the pages of this book.

Explorations

- Do Jung's experiences and theories have any relevance to your own experiences of the dream world?
- Have your important dreams sometimes seemed to balance out or compensate for limitations in your conscious perspective?
- Like Jung's experience with the subterranean temple, have any of your dream images differed from the imagery in your waking life? Is it possible that these images arose from a collective level of the unconscious different from your own personal unconscious?
- If you have sensed a guiding hand in your dream life, has that led you to wonder about another center of consciousness, a deeper self, distinct from your ego?
- Does Jung's concept of individuation have any meaning for you? Have you felt a sense of a progressive unfolding in your life, of an evolutionary urge that pushes you toward wholeness?
- Perhaps some of Jung's concepts have meaning to you and others don't. Which of his ideas fit for you? There is no right or wrong, only your own journey toward understanding your inner world.

CHAPTER THREE

Jane Roberts and the Multidimensional Soul

Jane Roberts, another courageous investigator of the dream world, came at dreams from a different angle than Carl Jung. One of the finest mediums of the twentieth century, Roberts channeled an intelligence called Seth who, over twenty years, described the structure of the universe and the multidimensional souls that inhabit it. Seth's teachings included a description of the dream world and the relationship between our waking and dreaming selves. The large body of information channeled by Roberts is known as the Seth Material.

Roberts's more speculative work is included here because it offers a possible, if unprovable, explanation of some of the more mysterious dreams presented in this book. These dreams include flying dreams, detailed dreams of other lifetimes, in-dream visitations and healings, otherworldly encounters, and precognitive dreams. Although we can never know for certain whether Seth was a sub-personality of Jane Roberts or an independent entity, the Seth Material is thought-provoking and offers a coherent framework for understanding our more extraordinary dreams.

Roberts herself was, by nature, intellectual and skeptical, and wanted to corroborate Seth's teachings. With this in mind, she participated in experiments to test Seth's ability to clairvoyantly know things beyond the range of her own senses. She also used her own dream life as a laboratory to test Seth's teachings. Her experiments in the dream world were rigorous, including periods where she recorded five dreams a night. Her experiments focused on developing greater conscious awareness while in the dream state and using the dream world to launch into other dimensions of reality.

A lifelong writer, Roberts left a legacy of written work describing different aspects of her investigations. She compiled several volumes of edited transcripts and commentary on the Seth Material. She also wrote fiction, science fiction, non-fiction, and poetry in her own voice. Her later writing often engaged with Sethian themes. Roberts' papers are archived at Yale University.

A Note on Mediumship

Before discussing Jane Roberts and the Seth Material, it's important to say a few words about mediumship. Since the beginning of human history, a small percentage of human beings have been able to access information and guidance from somewhere other than the conscious personality. Individuals with sensitivity to non-physical realities have had guides or non-physical teachers who have spoken to them while they were in the dream world or in a trance state. In the last chapter, we saw that Jung had such a relationship with Philemon. Sometimes these intuitive human beings have channeled teachings through automatic writing. Sometimes they have allowed their non-physical teachers to speak aloud, using their physical bodies.

Mediumship first appeared in shamanistic cultures throughout the pre-industrial world. These cultures used fasting, chanting, dancing, and sometimes drugs to induce trance. Shamans sometimes traveled into the dream world to receive information from animal guides and non-physical teachers. Some shamans allowed their non-physical teacher to speak through them.

Mediums were also highly valued in ancient Greece. Connected with the temples of different gods, mediums went into trance and delivered messages from the gods to their supplicants. Political and military leaders faithfully consulted with these oracles before making important decisions.

Impressive mediums have appeared in more recent history, including Emmanuel Swedenborg in eighteenth-century Sweden and Edgar Cayce in twentieth-century America. Jane Roberts, a twentieth-century woman with modern views, channeled teachings known for their lack of religious bias.

Early History

As is the case with many people sensitive to other dimensions of reality, Jane Roberts's childhood in Saratoga, New York was filled with challenge and loss. Her father left when she was an infant, leaving welfare checks and a string of housekeepers to hold the family together. When she was very young, Roberts became the primary caretaker for her embittered, abusive mother, who was bedridden with rheumatoid arthritis. Social services became involved with the Roberts family, and during one of her mother's hospitalizations, Roberts was removed from her home and placed in an orphanage, where she spent two years.

From age five, Roberts knew she was going to be a writer and that she wanted to devote her life to her work. She said of herself that she wrote everywhere and anywhere, and that she felt safest while sitting on her back porch, writing.[15]

An Unexpected Revelation

In 1963, when she was thirty-four years old, Jane Roberts was living with her husband, Robert Butts, in Elmira, New York. She was a poet and fiction writer, and he was an artist. While both of them were inspired by nature and the arts, neither was interested in metaphysics or religion. Although Roberts had been raised Catholic by her mother, she had questioned many of the beliefs of Catholicism as she grew older, and had moved away from the Church.

Given the agnostic views that Roberts shared with her husband, she couldn't have been more surprised when, in 1963, she entered an altered state of consciousness as she sat at her writing desk. During this life-changing experience, a very different world view was downloaded into her consciousness, "a gut knowing, a biological knowledge." Here's how Roberts described this experience:

> What happened next was like a "trip" without drugs. If someone had slipped me an LSD cube on the side, the experience couldn't have been more bizarre. Between one normal minute and the next, a fantastic avalanche of radical, new ideas burst into my head with tremendous force, as if my skull were come sort of receiving station, turned up to unbearable volume. Not only ideas came though this channel, but sensations, intensified and pulsating. I was tuned in, turned on—whatever you want to call it—connected to some incredible source of energy, I didn't even have time to call out to Rob.[16]

With her devotion to the written word, Roberts struggled to keep pace with the concepts pouring through her. She later transcribed close to a hundred pages of typewritten notes that upended her previously firm belief that we are formed exclusively from physical matter and that the only existing world is the physical one. This experience challenged her previously held beliefs and changed her life.

> As it was, I didn't know what had happened, yet even then I felt that my life had suddenly changed. The word "revelation" came to mind and I tried to dismiss it, yet the word was apt. I was simply afraid of the word with its mystical implications. I was familiar with inspiration in my own work, but this was as different from ordinary inspiration as a bird is from a worm![17]

Roberts's revelatory experience brought the world of paranormal experience to her attention for the first time. Soon after, she submitted a proposal to write a book on extrasensory perception, the ways we receive information other than through our physical senses. This was a topic about which Roberts knew next to nothing. Much to her surprise, she was offered a publishing contract.

One of the chapters of Roberts's book was on the use of Ouija boards to contact the spirit world. Neither she nor her husband had ever operated one before. In the process of exploring the Ouija board for the book, they encountered an intelligence that called himself Seth.

Seth first presented himself through the moving pointer, but Roberts soon began to hear his words before they were spelled out. Although she was initially frightened, she soon felt relieved when she spoke the words damming up inside her. After a few sessions of moving back and forth between the Ouija board and speaking directly for Seth, Roberts abandoned the Ouija board, and became the conduit for Seth. To act as a medium, she went into a trance that allowed her to disconnect from her conscious personality. Seth, with his different personality and his different views, was then able to speak through her.[18]

At the beginning, both Roberts and her husband were certain Seth must be a sub-personality of Roberts. However, as Seth's presence became stronger, his differences from her became more pronounced. In addition to his different viewpoints, his sense of humor, physical gestures, and voice were unlike those of Roberts. These differences were noted by Butts, who remained fully conscious and interactive during the sessions with Seth. Because Butts was able to observe the differences between Seth and his wife, he soon became convinced that Seth was far more than a sub-personality. Roberts, who couldn't observe herself as she channeled Seth, didn't have this additional perspective and found it more difficult to accept Seth as an independent being.[19]

The Importance of Robert Butts

Just as Toni Wolff was essential to the birth of Jungian psychology, Robert Butts was essential to the birthing of the Seth Material. Seth stated that Roberts and Butts were aspects of the same soul, working together to deliver these teachings. Although this assertion is unprovable, it is clear that Robert Butts was crucial to the creation of the Seth Material.

While Roberts channeled Seth, Butts tracked the outside world and provided the ongoing connection with physical reality that Roberts gave up while in trance. It is likely that this grounding allowed Roberts to detach with greater ease from the physical world and to open more fully to Seth.

Butts took notes at every session and later transcribed them, creating the record of the Seth sessions. These notes provided the raw material for all of the Seth books. Butts and Robert also studied these notes together and developed an understanding of viewpoints that were initially foreign to them. Finally, as already noted, both Roberts and Butts participated in the investigation of the dream world. On many levels, Butts provided the companionship, grounding, and security that allowed the Seth Material to emerge.

A few basic concepts can act as a doorway to this complex body of work left to us through the efforts of this couple.

A Multidimensional Soul in a Multidimensional Universe

Many of us believe that the three-dimensional, physical world is the only existing world and that we are strictly biological creatures. We believe that our five senses access the one and only objective world. Seth taught otherwise. In his view, a human being is a sub-personality of a powerful, dynamic immortal soul. This soul has split off into countless fragments or sub-personalities in order to advance its experience and knowledge. Seth said of our soul:

> The trouble is that you frequently consider the soul or entity as a finished, static "thing" that belongs to you but is not you. The soul or entity—in other words, your most intimate powerful inner identity—is and must be forever changing. It is not, therefore, something like a cherished heirloom. It is alive, responsive, curious. It forms the flesh and the world that you know, and it is in a state of becoming.[20]

The various forms which the soul takes on in the course of its development include our physical world as we now know it, re-incarnational dramas in other time periods, the dream world, probable realities that are variations of our current three-dimensional reality, and non-physical dimensions of reality.

From the Sethian viewpoint, our soul has created the physical body with its physical senses in order to have a particular experience. Because our physical senses can only perceive the physical world, we believe it to be the only reality. As we become more interested in and explore non-physical realties, we can learn more about the true nature of the universe and our soul.

The Dream World

Seth viewed our waking physical world and our dream world as intertwined. We solve problems of waking life in our dreams. We also create important experiences that our conscious personalities are missing in waking life. In the dream world, we utilize meaningful, personal metaphors to create these needed experiences. When we attend to our dreams, we can receive useful information about our physical and emotional health. These particular views of Seth overlap with some schools of contemporary psychology. However, this overlap is a small part of Seth's teachings.

For Seth, the dream world was not just an imaginary state or a repository for things unacceptable to our waking selves. Rather, the dream world is another dimension of reality with its own unique molecular structure and its own laws.

> The dream world has a molecular structure, but this construction takes up no space as you know it. The dream world consists of depth and dimensions, expansions and contractions that are more clearly related, perhaps to ideals that have no need for the particular kind of structure with which you are familiar. The intuitions and certain other inner abilities have so much more freedom here that it is unnecessary for molecules to be used in any kind of imprisoning form. Action in the dream world is more fluid. The images

> appear and disappear much more quickly because value fulfillment is allowed greater reign.[21]

Although we remember some of our dreams and are consciously helped by them, we create many other dreams that lie outside our awareness. Our dream life continues to unfold while we are in waking life, and our dreams help us in ways of which we simply are ignorant. One reason that our dreams can seem chaotic and fragmentary is that we drop into the dream world in mid-dream and remember only small portions of it.

Another important aspect of Seth's theory was that every dream is an electromagnetic event that leaves its mark on us. Just as our waking experiences are encoded in our body and psyche, so are our dream experiences. When we die, the encoded experiences of our waking and dreaming lives survive death and are absorbed by our soul.

The Inner Senses

In addition to physical senses that process the material world, Seth described another set of senses he called the *inner senses*.[22] Five of the most important of these inner senses are (1) inner vibrational touch, (2) psychological time (Psi-Time), (3) perception of past, present and future, (4) the conceptual sense, and (5) cognition of knowledgeable essence. We use these senses to perceive realties other than our three-dimensional physical world. When we dream, we switch from the outer senses to the inner senses. Our outer senses are quiescent and we are focused on the input of our inner senses.

Psychological time is a state of consciousness that allows us to move flexibly between the inner and the outer senses, and sometimes to experience them simultaneously. *Inner vibrational touch* is an inner sense that allows us to experience deep empathic knowing of the experience of living things—people, plants, and animals. *Perception of past, present, and future* offers an instantaneous knowing of the past, present, and future of beings we encounter. *The conceptual sense* allows us to merge with the total electrical and chemical composition of concepts and to experience those concepts fully, not just as mental ideas. *The cognition of knowable essence* is the ability to penetrate the boundary that encloses another and to know the essence of that being.[22]

The Three Dream Bodies

Seth distinguished three different bodies that we use when we're not in the physical world. These bodies are essentially different states of consciousness, but the perception of a body allows us to maintain a sense of identity as we travel in other dimensions of reality. As we move deeper into inner space and farther away from the physical body, more of the inner senses are activated.

Our first dream body is the one most of us recognize from our dreams. This body navigates the dream world. With this body, we are able to perceive past, present, and future in the physical world. We also have limited ability to levitate and fly.

In our second form, we leave physical limitation behind. We are able to walk through walls and to levitate easily, flying out into our solar system, but not beyond. In this body, we have meetings with other beings in the dream world.

In the third body, we are farthest away from the limitations of the physical body. This is the true out-of-body consciousness in which we explore the past, present, and future of other dimensions of reality.[23]

Training and Projection Naps

In the Sethian universe, part of waking consciousness is tasked with navigating the physical world. This aspect of our waking self is unable to leave the physical world. However, other parts of our waking consciousness can be trained to become more flexible and can learn to navigate realities other than the physical world. This kind of conscious navigation in other realities is known as out-of-body projection.

Though Roberts experimented with projecting out-of-body from the waking state, she found this alarming. Learning to launch from the dream state where she was already detached from the physical body created a gentler launching pad for her out-of-body explorations. In service of intentional out-of-body travel, Roberts and Butts took short "projection naps." They set their intention to become consciously aware that they were dreaming and to levitate out of the dream body for travel into other dimensions of reality.

One day as Roberts was taking a projection nap, she found herself in a beautiful garden talking to her husband. The details of her experience were so clear that she couldn't tell whether she was sleeping or dreaming. In order to determine if she was awake or dreaming, she willed herself to levitate, something she couldn't do if she were awake. She had the following extraordinary experience.

> At once, my feet and legs felt very strange, filled with a rustling sensation. There was a funny sense of inner shifting. Suddenly, I saw many mirrors, which I knew weren't physical and didn't belong in the room. I was propelled through them with amazing speed. There were scenes within the mirrors, and people moving about. I rushed through a series of such scenes. The traveling sensations were very real, indisputable, and somewhat frightening.
>
> I "landed" on a hillside. Two women ran over the hills, and I followed them. I had no idea who the

> women were, but I decided to see whether I could leap from the ground in this state to the top of one of the hills. As soon as I thought of this, I sped up through the air to the top, then backward to where I had been standing. To make sure of my results, I executed the same leap once again.[24]

Roberts reported another powerful experience from this time of intensive experimentation:

> During this period, of course, we were recording all the dreams we could capture. Usually at least one of mine per night dealt with flying or levitation. During a series of dreams, I seemed to be working to perfect my "flying technique," and was taking lessons from others. Then, in the middle of several dreams such as this, I dreamed the following, according to my notes:
>
> The whole dream was in images. I saw the universe, or whole reality, an infinity of spirals and stars, in multi-dimensional depth. Someone told me that most of our cherished ideas about the nature of reality were completely wrong. This was a revelation-type dream but I couldn't remember much of it at all upon awakening. Someone was guiding me, I believe.[25]

Precognitive Dreams

Roberts tracked many kinds of dreams, but none with more interest than her precognitive dreams. These dreams had special interest to her because they validated the existence of inner senses perceiving things that haven't yet appeared in our waking reality.

Of course, Roberts couldn't know when she first had a dream if it would prove to be precognitive, and sometimes her precognitive dreams weren't particularly significant to her. Later, when it became apparent that happenings in the outer world had already appeared in a dream, she carefully compared the details of her dream—place, character, and action—with the details of the outer world event.

Although many of Roberts's precognitive dreams were about relatively unimportant things, she was naturally very interested in precognitive dreams connected to her own destiny. In a three-year period in the 1960s, she tracked a series of precognitive dreams connected to her attempts to find a publisher for her work. At the time, her book on ESP had been published and she was working on two new books—one on the Seth material and one on dreams. The first dream occurred in 1966.

> On February 12, 1966, I dreamed that I was on a bed, with Rob on one side of me and another man nearby. There was no pain but a movement in the pelvis, and I delivered a baby. But the doctor held up two infants, and I thought with a laugh, "Oh, no! Twins. This is really two much!"—meaning that after having no children, two at once was really something. Then the doctor reassured me that only one baby was involved. The hospital was in my own childhood neighborhood. I was pleased that the delivery was easy and painless.[26]

Upon awakening, Roberts had no idea of the meaning of the dream. Seth, whose skills included dream interpretation, suggested to her that the babies might be about two creative projects that would prove to be one. Roberts was interested in this interpretation, but continued to try to find a publisher for the two books she was working on—one on dreams and one on Seth.

Over the following couple of years, Roberts had many dreams that revealed the step-by- step fate of her submissions.

They accurately predicted the specific disappointments she would encounter.

In the late spring of 1968, Roberts sent her dream book to Prentice, and had the following dream:

> *Then I saw a letter about my book from Prentice. It was on normal typing paper and requested, first, some further work on the book—either an outline of a projected book to include portions of the dream manuscript but stressing Seth, or some sample chapters—before a contract would be signed. One sentence read, "Or better, send on some notes from the original Seth material, and maybe we can consider this as advance work for a contract."*[27]

On May 5, Roberts received a note from Prentice asking for a prospectus with Seth's views on several topics, suggesting that this would be the basis for a contract—just as her dream had predicted. Her proposal to them had been about dreams, not about Seth. Her dream accurately predicted this requested shift in emphasis from dreams to Seth's teachings.

On receiving this letter, Roberts assumed that she needed to go through the forty or so notebooks of Seth Material to produce the prospectus. She began the work with a heavy heart, since she didn't really want to do this kind of work until she had a contract.

On May 14, she had a dream that she wasn't handling the prospectus correctly. She was so upset that she called Prentice. She discovered that she had misunderstood the letter and only needed to submit a simple prospectus and outline. This dream and her subsequent call to Prentice saved her many hours of work. She was able to get what was needed off in the mail within a couple of days.

Roberts did eventually sign a contract with Prentice and, in 1970, she published *The Seth Material,* a book that combined her original two books—the dream manuscript and the Seth material. The twins did turn out to be one baby, just as her initial dream years before had predicted.[28]

Seth and the Development of Human Consciousness

As we have seen, in the Sethian universe, the multidimensional soul creates new experiences for itself through sub-personalities that exist in many dimensions. Those sub-personalities are also able to evolve within the lines of development of their own realities.

As we humans develop, we learn that the physical world is not the only reality. As we explore the dream world and other non-physical realities, we learn to identify less with the limitations of the physical senses. We experience expansive, wondrous realities and become more identified with our limitless, multidimensional soul.

Jane Roberts dictated the following poem to Robert Butts from her hospital bed, six months before she died. This poem describes the experience open to us as we develop.

> My history is filled
> with kingdoms lost and kingdoms found,
> with magic mirrors that open up
> into brand-new cosmic maps,
> and within my head
> glittering worlds are spread
> enough to fill
> a thousand books.
> Multiple vision leads me on
> over paths that form
> new worlds of fact.[29]

Recap and Moving Forward

The first three chapters of this book provide different lenses for understanding the dreams that follow. In the first chapter, we looked at the ultimate mystery of dreams and some tools used by modern dreamworkers. We then examined the life and conceptual understandings of two extraordinary explorers of the dream world.

We saw that both Carl Jung and Jane Roberts believed that the waking self is not the true center of our personality. For Jung, the true center is the self, an archetype that lies deep in the collective unconscious. As we develop, different aspects of our selves are activated by this true center of our lives. Later in his life, Jung suggested that the self, as well as other archetypes, are *psychoid*—that is, they are both physiological and psychological in nature.[30]

Although Jung's own experiences raised metaphysical questions, he was intent on making a substantial contribution to the field of psychology. He focused on how dreams, visions, and other psychological events are connected to our individuation. He trusted in the psychological development that emerges from an active dialogue between our conscious and unconscious, our dreams and our waking consciousness.

Seth, as channeled by Jane Roberts, also located the true center of our personality outside of our waking self. According to Seth, we are multidimensional souls, currently creating and exploring countless realities. The dream world like the physical world is an objective place, with its own molecular structure. We can explore other dimensions beyond the waking and dream worlds through out-of-body projection.

Seth, like Jung, believed that the dream world is linked to our waking selves and that our dreams can provide useful information about the next steps in our development. However, for Seth, the interactions between our waking selves and the dream world are a very small part of the multidimensional universe.

In the upcoming chapters, we look at different kinds of dreams offered by people committed to working with their dreams. These dreams are beautiful, powerful offerings from the unconscious. This book focuses on the developmental contributions of our dreams, how they help us to become more fully our selves throughout our lifetimes. In this sense, the primary perspective of the book resonates with Jungian thought. However, the theory of archetypes may not be the most elegant explanation of flying dreams, re-incarnational dramas, visitations, precognitive dreams, or in-dream healings. When these kinds of dreams are presented in the book, the Seth Material is referenced.

Explorations

- Have you had dreams that seem more than metaphorical and more like travels in another dimension?
- Have you had precognitive dreams or dreams where you seem to be flying into different dimensions of reality?
- Have you experienced dream visits with others that seem more like a dream visitation than a dream drama?
- Have you had dreams which seemed more like re-incarnational dramas rather than normal dream dramas? What makes these dreams seem different than normal dream dramas?
- Begin to track these different kinds of dreams.
- With precognitive dreams, compare details of the dream—place, characters, and action—with the waking event.
- If you're interested in exploring out-of-body experiences in dreams, find a teacher and research the feedback about this teacher. Out-of-body travel can be challenging. Receiving support and instruction is important.

Chapter Four

Early Illuminations

Most of the experiences of our childhoods have receded into an impenetrable fog. When our childhood dreams are powerful enough to slip through that fog, they more than likely were connected to central experiences in our young lives. These dreams may have offered solace or a frightening snapshot of our situation. They may have offered needed experiences our childhood lacked or may have focused us on how to handle difficulties. Most likely those early remembered dreams were filled with strong emotion: terror, joy, or sadness. They affected us as deeply as the few outer events that we can retrieve from those early years and we have never forgotten them.

Although we remember these early dreams because of their initial impact, we also remember them because of their connection to our unfolding destiny. They revealed important aspects of our character and life themes that were starting to appear. In retrospect, we understand that we held onto those dreams because they were lights that illuminated our life path. They were harbingers of what was to come.

Jungian analyst Kate Marcus wrote the following about the early dreams and fantasies found in the autobiographies of creative people. Her insight can be applied to the experience of many people, whether or not they have written an autobiography:

> When we read an autobiography of an outstanding person, we often find there an early dream or fantasy that has the quality of a psychological landmark. Not infrequently we then get the impression that only this person would have remembered this experience throughout this life. He has not discarded it as a childish fantasy but has allowed it to remain with him as a light illuminating his path. The closer a person has lived to the creative unconscious, the closer he often feels to that which he remembers from far back.[31]

As we will see, our early dreams, the ones that stay with us for a lifetime, contain many different kinds of images of our future unfolding.

Realistic and Fantastical Images in Early Dreams

A study by Kelly Bulkeley and a team of dream researchers offers an interesting picture of the content of the earliest dreams we remember.[34] Bulkeley and his team interviewed 109 people living in a rural area in the northeastern part of the United States. Their extensive interviews included the question: "What is the earliest dream you can remember, whether it was last month, last year or many years ago?" The participants ranged from fifteen to eighty-eight. This study found that 78% of the participants remembered dreams they had between three and twelve years old.[32]

One of their findings was in regard to fantastical imaginary and religious elements. Although there were slightly more realistic dreams that resembled outer happenings, there were almost as many dreams with fantasy elements. These dreams included bizarre settings and fantastical characters like the "boogeyman" or Frankenstein's monster. More fantastically oriented dreams also included ghosts and haunted houses, and religious figures such as Mary and Jesus. The researchers commented that these fantasy elements seem to be more present in remembered childhood dreams than in adult dreams.

The childhood dreams in this book were dreamed by children between three and ten. The dreams are both realistic and fantastical. A sequence of flying dreams and a dream about World War II might be considered within the Sethian framework as an out-of-body experience and a re-incarnational drama, respectively. Each of the shared dreams deeply affected the young dreamer. Like Carl Jung's childhood dream of a subterranean temple, these early dreams revealed important things about the child's character and her unique destiny. They were early signs of the dreamer's unique process of unfolding.

Encounter with a Witch

In my own life, my first memory is a fantastical dream that occurred when I was around three. As is the case in dreams of very young children, there was very little plot line. Instead my dream presented a terrifying otherworldly image as well as a snapshot of my emotional relationship with my mother.

> *In the dream I awaken and find a hideous witch in the cream-colored rocker in the corner of my room. I'm terrified but have nowhere to run since my mother's bed doesn't feel safe. I'm paralyzed by fear, with no good options. Finally, I head toward my mother's bed, not a good choice, but the best one I have.*

Almost a half-century later, that dream still had enough power to inspire the following poem:

Midnight Choices

I startle awake and she's there
crouched in the corner of my room,

hair yellow and frizzed
her eyes hungry crows.

One mole rises from her chin
like a dab of tar,

I'm three, her cackle echoes
with black intent.

Small twitching girl
I scan my choices,

slide bare feet to the floor
and creep toward mother's bed,

a place already known,
cold as ice.

This dream was my first memory as well as my first remembered experience of something not of this world, and I was filled with terror. I was also filled with awe. The dream left me with the visceral conviction that there are things in the universe that we can't see in waking life and that we can connect with those otherworldly things in dreams. Looking back from the perspective of a long life, I can see that this dream was a first indicator of my lifelong quest to understand invisible spiritual realities.

My dream also clearly presented a psychological dilemma. I needed my mother and yet found her cold and frightening. I made the best choice I could, but it wasn't a happy one. This in-dream dilemma presented a difficult emotional truth that would haunt my childhood.

At the time of this dream, my mother, my father, and I were living in an apartment in Pittsburgh, Pennsylvania. My father was a lawyer. My mother, a homemaker, was pregnant with her second child. By this time in her life, my mother had suffered many disappointments and losses. She had fallen into a profound depression when her fiancé was killed in World War II. Many of her earlier dreams and aspirations were also thwarted. Like millions of other women who worked in factories or received good educations during the war, her hopes and ambitions disappeared after the men returned. Although she had been well educated, she was expected to be fulfilled as a homemaker and mother, like Donna Reed and other cheerful housewives on T.V.

The life force of my beautiful, intelligent mother had been blocked, and she was angry. I encountered her rage and felt responsible for her lost dreams. By the time I was three, I was well acquainted with the witch, the dark side of feminine power. My dream clearly presented the insecurity I felt with her.

My witch dream clarified my situation in a way I never forgot and presented the wound I would need to heal. Shortly after that dream, I began to establish a series of relationships with surrogate mothers—my grandmothers, teachers, and neighborhood moms. As a young adult, I found a mentor who recognized my psychological talents and found me my first job as a psychiatric aide in a mental hospital. And I eventually found a good therapist who helped me to unravel the complicated ties with my mother and to gain confidence in myself.

In defining my major life issue, my dream was also connected to my professional life. I learned through my own healing how the healing process works, and then helped many men and women with their early wounding. My first dream, in presenting my own psychological circumstances, presaged both my own lifelong healing and the professional work I would do as a psychotherapist and as a mentor and teacher of other therapists.

Glenna Travels to her Grandmother's Farm

Unlike my witch dream, which was fantastical and brought a painful, real-life problem to my attention, Glenna Berry Horton's dream of returning to her grandmother's farm was a reality-based dream that brought solace and hope.

Glenna is a poet, publisher, and avocado farmer who lives in San Luis Obispo and Carpinteria, California. As a child she lived with her parents, sister, and two brothers on a farm in Iowa. Each summer, she and her family traveled to her grandmother's farm in Nebraska. The contrast between life at these two farms was one of the central features of her childhood.

Of life in Iowa, Glenna remembers extremes of heat in summer and cold in winter, hard physical work, and frequent illness in her family. She and her siblings were ill so often that her home had a special sick room for the kids. After age four, when she had ear and tonsil problems, she spent a lot of time in that room.

Glenna's summer vacations in Nebraska were very different. The family left work and sweltering heat behind. Her hard-working father rested and the kids, freed from the labors of de-tasseling corn, swam in the river and ran free. In contrast to Iowa, Nebraska was a place of health and freedom as well as immersion in the love of her grandparents.

Glenna's recurring dream of traveling to her grandmother's farm began at the same time as her childhood illnesses and lasted until she was a young adult. Her dreams and fantasies about Nebraska helped her survive the lonely times in the sick room and reminded her of good times to come. She dreamed this particular dream-within-a-dream when she was six or seven.

> *My parents have just driven the eight hours from hot steamy River Bottom, Iowa to my grandmother's farm in high, dry Nebraska. When my grandparents come to embrace us, they lift us out of the car in darkness and a cooling breeze comes through the back seat. It is heavenly! Because we are fussy from the ride, my grandparents brings out wooden wagons to ride us kids around and calm us before bed.*
>
> *I fall asleep to the creaking of the wagon and dream about the summer ahead, filled with the peonies, irises, zinnias and asters my grandmother grew. I dream about wading in the lily pond with the fish scooting through my toes. I dream about the beautiful, but vicious rooster I saved from my grandfather's ax and about the chicks I raised from eggs. When I wake up from the dream within a dream, I'm being carried to my wrought-iron bed, I'm delighted to think that this dream will turn to real life throughout the summer.*

In speaking of this dream, Glenna noted the theme of happiness and bliss at the end of the difficult car trip. This theme provided her with the understanding that every adventure has hard times that lead up to rewards and happiness. This understanding of life has stayed with her and has given her a framework to meet challenges.

These recurring dreams also prefigured the importance of a sanctuary connected to the land and agriculture. Both her summers in Nebraska and her dreams about the summer provided solace and created a lifelong template of valuing sanctuary and respite from work. As a young mother with small children,

Glenna's sanctuary was an hour to herself in a car parked in a wooded area. Still later in life, she married a man who owned an avocado ranch. She and her husband worked hard at jobs in San Luis Obispo, but traveled south to rest at the family avocado ranch in Carpinteria. There they slowed down, visiting with friends, children, and grandchildren. Glenna's early dreams of travel to her grandmother's farm were part of the emergence of a lifelong pattern of hard work followed by retreat to a sanctuary closely connected to the earth and agriculture.

Prartho Flies

Unlike Glenna's childhood dreams, which offered the solace of earthly pleasures, Prartho Sereno's early flying dreams provided otherworldly comfort as she floated out into the stars. Prartho, a poet and teacher who lives in Marin County, California, says that she never told anyone about these dreams: "They didn't belong to the world I shared with others, and I don't think I had the language to describe them. Even now that's true. Poetry is the best I can do."

The following poem describes her early flying experiences:

Sailing, Three Years Old

I don't remember what it was that got
me up from bed to float in my pajamas
down the upstairs hallway to the window
at the end—the leaded one with beveled glass
that scattered daylight on the hardwood floor.

But I do remember the jump
through that window—out into the stars
where I sailed, briefly held, before
drifting down to the gravel below.

I loved the weightless part, but also
coming back into the shapes and smells
of the earth—hedges and rooftops,
the pile of neighborkids' bikes
heaped where they'd been dropped.
The crunch of stones beneath my feet.

And I loved the dome of loneliness
I drifted through, a private observatory
for looking in on the world, which was,
for this little while, mine.
Then I took the stairs back up (who knows
how? Surely the doors were locked)
and got into bed. I did this every night
for weeks on end, and nobody ever noticed.[33]

Prartho experienced her flying dreams throughout her childhood in Rochester, New York. They were consistent with her dislike of confinement and with the adventurous spirit she had exhibited since birth. Her mother told stories about the daring baby who climbed from her crib and the toddler who slipped through fences. When asked if her flying dreams scared her, she answered, "Not at all. Just about everything about the waking world was scary. This was an experience of utter joy, grace, and freedom."

That Prartho sought out the "dome of loneliness" in the dream world may be related to being the middle child of five. Although she remembers her family as harmonious as a large family can be, she was sensitive and was affected by the tensions and complications of family life. The worry she saw on the adults' faces frightened her. The experiences of solitude, offered by her dreams, provided needed relief from the overstimulation in a large family.

These early dreams also revealed the adventurous and spiritually inclined nature that would shape many of her later choices. From her late teens until she was fifty, she lived what she calls an "itinerant" life. She moved many times on the east coast and west coast, and lived in India for a time. Her diverse jobs included taxi driver, restaurant manager, tarot reader, psychotherapist, and community college teacher. She lived on a farm and in the city. She lived as a single woman and then as a mother with two daughters. In keeping with her lifelong interest in spiritual matters, she spent her forties in a spiritual community.

Prartho says of her flying dreams that she's not sure that they were dreams in the usual sense. The details of her home and yard as she flew out into the stars were realistic. She believes that a subtle part of herself may have slipped free of her body and enjoyed her nighttime adventures. Her understanding of this flying experience resonates with Seth's description of a dream body that can levitate from our normal dream state and fly out into the universe.

Regardless of the interpretation of Prartho's flying dreams, they were harbingers of the life to come. Her flying dreams have continued throughout her life. As an adult, she still frolics in the ethers without the weight of a physical body. "It's almost like swimming," she says. When these dreams come, she feels joyous and remembers that she is more than a physical body and that the universe has many levels of reality.

Laurel Attempts to Save the Children

In addition to the fantastical or mythological and more realistic dreams mentioned in Bulkeley's study, children also dream of life circumstances quite different than their current ones. Are these dreams woven from images seen on television or movies? Are these images picked up from the unconscious of parents or from memories stored in the collective unconscious? Or are these images glimpses into other re-incarnational dramas? While we can't know the ultimate answer to these questions, we do know that children have vivid, detailed dreams of life situations very different from their current ones. These dreams can be centered around emotional dilemmas unrelated to what they have experienced thus far in life. Like our other childhood dreams, these can set the stage for the unfolding of the dreamer's life.

Laurel Connell is a forty-year-old mother of two who works as a psychotherapist in Ventura County, California. When Laurel was ten, she had the following dream:

> *I'm living in a time in the midst of a war. I would say World War II without hesitation. In the dream, however, I'm an adult. Whether I'm male or female, I don't know. I'm working along with a partner, who is a woman, and we're on a mission.*
>
> *We're very focused on rescuing children and getting them to safety. There's a cellar, that seems like it's dug out of the earth. It smells of soil and feels damp to my skin. There are benches that have been built into the walls of the cellar, but very basic wooden boards that run the length of the walls.*
>
> *My partner and I are quick in our movements, as we are carrying children down a ladder into the cellar. As she goes down, I am next to go up. We quickly deposit the children onto the earthen floor and swiftly climb the ladder to retrieve another child. The feeling I have is that of intensity and purpose. I'm concerned that we're running out of time. Each child brought down is a victory.*
>
> *But then, my partner and I make a disastrous realization. There's a bomb either down in the shelter or in very close proximity to the cellar. We look at one another and understand that we must immediately begin to carry all of the children back up and out at once. Each of us is only able to take one at a*

time. No words are spoken between us at any time in the dream. It is an understanding we have together and we communicate with our eyes.

As I climb down to retrieve another child, after I have brought one or two up above, the bomb detonates. I immediately die and am aware that I have lost my life. In the dream, I am aware that my life is over and I'm on the other side. It's all black, almost as though I am in outer space, floating. I'm peaceful, light, neutral. Floating through blackness, darkness, but moving towards something. And then I hear a voice telling me, "Open your mouth." I wake up.

At the time that Laurel had this dream, she was living in an old Victorian on the outskirts on Philadelphia. Both of her parents were healers. Her father, a chiropractor, and her mother, a massage therapist, had offices in one half of their Victorian. Laurel, her younger brother, and her parents lived in the other half of the house. Laurel remembers her parents as continually engaged with some form of personal or spiritual growth. Reincarnation was an accepted belief in the household. Unlike the violence and desperate circumstances experienced in her dream, Laurel's life in Philadelphia felt safe and secure. She knew she was loved and felt encouraged to express herself freely. The trauma of war was far removed from her life.

At age ten, when Laurel had her dream, she thought it was "cool." She knew that her dream self was living through a different life experience. This dream gave her a powerful and never forgotten verification of the views her parents espoused. This dream set the stage for later becoming a student at a Buddhist university and her belief in multidimensional and spiritual realities.

Laurel's deeper connections to this dream emerged gradually. As a teenager, she was drawn to France. She developed a passion for the French language and went to France three times as a young adult. At 15, during her first trip, she wandered around the streets of Paris, imagining what it was like to be alive there during World War II. With her belief in other lives, she now wonders if her dream experience occurred in France and if she was drawn to France in an unconscious attempt to integrate her dream and that other incarnational experience.

The dilemma of this dream and its intense feelings became more relevant to Laurel when she was in her early twenties and caring for her two young children. At that time, she and her husband suffered a profound crisis that lasted for several years. Family members and friends died. Her husband lost his job and they went into a financial crisis. Laurel had not yet created a career for herself, money was short, and she wondered if she would be able to provide for her children. Filled with shame and fear, she experienced a desperate need to save the children entrusted to her, the same experience that appeared in her early dream of World War II. As she began to reflect more closely on her early dream, she realized that her dream self was driven by fear and didn't notice clues that the shelter was unsafe. In spite of his best intentions, he had failed in his tasks. As the underlying themes of that early dream became clearer to her, that dream became a cautionary tale about staying alert in her current circumstances.

If one is drawn to a re-incarnational explanation, Laurel's early dream experience laid out a theme that has preoccupied her during at least two lifetimes—saving vulnerable children in situations of extreme stress. From a Sethian perspective, her dire situation in her twenties wasn't a punishment for past failures, but rather the opportunity to develop new capacities and different results. And, in fact, that is what happened. She and her husband survived the dark years. She developed a successful career and her family came through financial and emotional hardship intact.

If one isn't drawn to the reincarnation explanation, it could be said that at age ten, Laurel was given a powerful, metaphorical story with themes that would later occupy her life. This unforgettable childhood dream also provided her with an experience that helped consolidate her spiritual orientation.

As an addendum, Laurel talks slowly and deliberately when she speaks. She says about herself, "I move very slowly before I make a decision." Understood in the context of her early dream, she is committed to taking in all the information available and not making mistakes that can be deadly. Again, whether this is the legacy of another life, or something she is working on solely in this life, is ultimately a mystery. In any case, her early dream set her on the path of paying close attention to managing fear and paying attention to details that can determine whether or not one survives.

A Living Loop

The dreams in this chapter reflect the wide-ranging nature of childhood dreams. They can be terrifying or comforting, reality-based or fantastical. They can place our focus more firmly on challenges of our lives or can open up other dimensions of reality. Although our early remembered dreams vary in tone and intent, they share a commonality: They are early signs of our unique destiny. These dreams reveal our character and point to themes that will preoccupy us throughout life. We hold onto them, in part, because they are powerful signs of the potentialities that are beginning to develop and of our unique individuation process. Conversely, because these dreams are so impactful, we remember them, and they become part of the life we create. This living loop of "dream birthing life birthing dream birthing life" is part of our human story. In the next chapters, we will see how that loop plays out in different stages of life.

Explorations

- Search your memory for dreams or dream fragments from childhood. Write these dreams down in your dream journal. Reflect on these dream offerings with a fresh eye.
- Do you remember how you felt when you awoke from these dreams as a child? What feelings do you have now about them? Do they still scare or delight you? What are your associations now to these dream images?
- Were important aspects of your character revealed by your dream self's orientation and actions?
- Have the themes in your early dream been important to you over your lifetime?
- Can you see your unconscious speaking to you and prefiguring your soul's unfolding?
- If your dreams were speaking to you from early in your life, does this change your understanding of the unconscious and your life journey?

Chapter Five

The Big Ones That Change Us

Our important childhood dreams reveal much about our developing character and about themes that will preoccupy us throughout our lifetimes. They are early signs of our unique destiny. As our life unfolds, our dreams continue to light the way. Small, somewhat forgettable, dreams respond to the more insignificant experiences of our life. Important, unforgettable dreams help us to navigate life's more life dramatic changes as something new within us presses for expression. Step by step, dream by dream, we manifest the potentials that are part of our destiny. Slowly, we become more truly ourselves and more whole. Jung called this process *individuation.* Rumi, the thirteenth-century Persian poet, wrote about our growing wholeness:

> A new moon teaches gradualness
> and deliberation and how one gives birth
> to oneself slowly. Patience with small details
> makes perfect a large work, like the universe.
> What nine months of attention does for an embryo
> forty early mornings will do
> for your gradually growing wholeness.[34]

Big Dreams

The most significant dreams of our life transform us. They are growth spurts in the slow process that Rumi describes. When we go to sleep, we're living in one reality. In our dream, we encounter an image or dramatic scenario so compelling that when we awaken we've been shaken out of our old ways of perceiving and being.

Our transformative dream may be part of a change we've been trying to make, or it may initiate a change we weren't expecting at all. Our dream may increase our confidence about making a major change or may plunge us into confusion about how to move forward. Regardless of these differences, our most important dreams meet us at the gates of change and initiate a new cycle in our psyche's unfolding.

Carl Jung called these important dreams "big" dreams and wrote the following about them:

> Not all dreams are of equal importance. Even primitives distinguish between "little" and "big" dreams, or, as we might say, "insignificant" and "significant" dreams. Looked at more closely, "little" dreams are the nightly fragments of fantasy coming from the subjective and personal sphere, and their meaning is limited to the affairs of everyday. That is why such dreams are easily forgotten, just because their validity is restricted to the day-to-day fluctuations of the psychic balance. Significant dreams, on the other hand, are remembered for a lifetime, and not infrequently prove to be the richest jewel in the treasure-house of psychic experience.[35]

Jung and the Study of Science

Jung, as we have seen in previous chapters, understood big dreams not just from his interaction with his patients, but from a lifelong engagement with his own life-changing dreams. Two paired big dreams came close together when he was about to enter university and helped him decide to pursue science. Up until the time he had these dreams, he was confused about how to move forward, given his many interests in both science and the humanities.

> In the first dream I was in a dark wood that stretched along the Rhine. I came to a little hill, a burial mound, and began to dig. After awhile I turned up, to my astonishment, some bones of prehistoric animals. This interested me enormously, and at that moment, I knew: I must get to know nature, the world in which we live, and the things around us.
>
> Then came a second dream. Again I was in a wood; it was threaded with watercourses, and in the darkest place I saw a circular pool, surrounded by dense undergrowth. Half immersed in the water lay the strangest and most wonderful creature: a round animal, shimmering in opalescent hues, and consisting of innumerable little cells, or of organs shaped like tentacles. It was a giant radiolarian, measuring three feet across. It seemed to me indescribably wonderful that this magnificent creature should be lying there undisturbed, in the hidden place, in the clear, deep water. It aroused in me an intense desire for knowledge, so that I awoke with a beating heart.[36]

Jung's dreams met him at the gateway between childhood and becoming a university student. His dreams helped him to navigate this transition by pointing him toward the course of study which ultimately led to medicine and his profession as a psychiatrist. Also clear in this dream was his attraction to things hidden in the depths—bones deep in the earth of a dark forest, and a semi-mythical creature in a deep pool, also in a forest. These dreams helped Jung make an immediate life decision but also presaged his interest in exploring the depths of the unconscious as a scientific discipline.

Kathleen Sullivan and The Trapped Eagle

One of the most compelling big dreams I've encountered appears in Kathleen Sullivan's *Recurring Dreams: A Journey to Wholeness.* She titled this dream "Caught in the Web: The Eagle Dream."

> I'm on a field trip with my class. The kids ahead of me become very excited about something they see which is not yet visible to me. I run, responding to their pleas, "Hurry, Ms. Sully! See what we've found!"
>
> When I join them, I see an enormous spider's web at least eighteen feet in diameter. At first I think it is a gorgeous sight, an awesome display of nature. But then I notice the Eagle. She is inexorably caught, splayed wing-to-wing, with her regal head stretched to the left, totally entangled in this spectacular web.
>
> Suddenly I experience grief so deep, so devastating, so all-consuming that I lose all the strength in my body. Falling to my knees, I sob from a place never before accessed. I am overcome by remorse, by despair.[37]

When Sullivan awoke from her dream, she was wracked with sobs. She was no stranger to nightmares, but the image of the trapped eagle captured the plight of her psyche. When she tried to distance herself from the dream during the following days, the dying eagle flashed before her eyes, refusing to be forgotten. When a well-meaning but misguided therapist asked her to visualize an easy extrication from the web, Sullivan's whole being shouted, "No," refusing the fix that was no fix at all for her. The trapped eagle had captured her attention and demanded that she do the hard work of extricating herself from the web of psychological patterns that was damaging her.

When Sullivan had this dream, she was in midlife with a successful teaching career, friends, and a home, but she was in trouble. Nightmares, headaches, fainting spells, outbursts of rage, and addictive patterns all indicated that something was off balance within her. Her dream encounter with the dying eagle cut through layers of denial. The eagle, a symbol of her own psyche trapped in complicated webs, brought her face to face with her own dire condition in a way she couldn't deny.

Out of this dream came a shift of orientation from denial to commitment to freeing the eagle. This commitment led Sullivan to therapy, recovery programs, study at the Esalen Institute, and an intensive engagement with her dreams. Particularly powerful was an evolving dream series that featured a young man she knew in high school. Sullivan called this series The Victor Biento Dream Series.

During these years of intensive psychological work, Sullivan drew on the image of the eagle to orient her journey. As she tackled different issues, she imagined herself cutting different strands of the web that imprisoned her.

The image of Sullivan's trapped eagle is powerful, a kind of poetry of the psyche. Jung wrote of the images that make our big dreams so evocative and transforming:

> They employ numerous mythological motifs that characterize the life of the hero, of that greater man who is semi-divine by nature. Here we find dangerous

> adventurers and ordeals such as occur in initiations. We meet dragons, helpful animals, and demons; also the Wise Old Man, the animal-man, the wishing tree, the hidden treasure, the cave, the walled garden, the transformative processes and substances of alchemy, and so forth—all things which in no way touch the banalities of everyday.[38]

In keeping with Jung's observation about the imagery in our big dreams, the next dream, "A Turtle Dream," includes a wise woman and a very lively turtle.

Denise's Turtle Dream

A resident of Eugene, Oregon, Denise M. Wallace has worked in the wine industry for twenty years, first as a manager of a tasting room and later as a sales rep. Denise has always loved wine, its flavors and aromas, its connections to culture and agriculture. In the past, she enjoyed helping clients to experience the pleasures of wine and to choose the right wines for their shops and special events. As her work shifted more to wholesale sales, the connection to the quality and the personal pleasure of wine became less important to her job, and she liked her work less.

Over time, the pressure of a job where she always had to be "on" also took its toll on her. She worked to balance her highly extroverted job with the quieter, more introverted side of herself through gardening and writing poetry. She tried to develop "a Buddhist sense of detachment" to deal with the ups and downs of being in sales. In spite of these ongoing efforts, she felt increasingly tired and unable to refuel. As she said, "I was not able to keep my inner cup full."

Although Denise was increasingly unhappy in her work life, it was difficult to contemplate a change. Her professional identity and financial well-being were tied up with her wine business and after many years of devoting herself to this work, she didn't have a clear idea of what she would do in place of it. Denise's big dream came in the middle of this difficult time and helped her to take the first step of a major life change. Here is Denise's turtle dream:

> *I'm in an outdoor setting like a shady garden or courtyard and a woman whose face I don't see, but whose presence is large and commanding, places a turtle in my hands about the size of a steering wheel!*
>
> *She tells me, "This turtle was a poet in his life, but now he's a turtle, and he is your responsibility."*
>
> *I ask, "Was he a famous poet?"*
>
> *"That doesn't matter," she says. "Just take really good care of him."*
>
> *I can feel the edges of the turtle's hard, damp shell against my palms, and also feel its soft underside. It wiggles its arms and legs and head as if fighting for its freedom, and then suddenly jumps out of my hands and runs away to hide under some foliage. I scramble after it, and after some searching, I hold it in my hands again, my thoughts racing about what to do to keep and protect it??*
>
> *Once again it leaps with some force out of my hands and disappears under some green, bushy plants. This time I can't find it, and am searching desperately when I wake up, filled with dread and loss, my throat tight and tears burning my eyes.*

Denise noted three major characters in her dream—a compelling woman, a turtle, and her dream self. The powerful woman who placed the turtle in her hands was mostly hidden in the shadows. She was a wise woman, perhaps a guide or the embodiment of Denise's deep self. Denise called her the bringer of information. She was a presence Denise couldn't fully see, as our deeper self always is. This wise woman initiated the action of the dream, giving Denise's dream self the task of caring for the turtle. For Denise, there could be comfort in knowing that something beyond her waking self was trying to help her.

The powerful and visceral focal point of Denise's dream was the agitated turtle that was determined to escape. Denise could feel its weight, the dryness of its shell. It was full of energy—wiggling, twisting its neck, desperately trying to escape from her. In the dream, and later when she worked on the dream, she resonated with its desperate desire to escape, so similar to her own feelings about her work life. As with Kathleen's experience with a trapped eagle, Denise's experience with a turtle embodied the state of her psyche in a palpable, undeniable way.

Although Denise's dream self understood that her task was to keep the turtle safe, she didn't know how to do it. In retrospect, the fact that the turtle escaped two times drove home the point of how badly he wanted to escape. That he was moving quickly, so unlike a turtle, also signaled his distress. At the end of the dream, when the turtle escaped, Denise was filled with a sense of sadness and dread. She hadn't taken proper care of her turtle and he was gone.

Denise's dialogue with the wise woman was also evocative. When the wise woman identified the turtle as a poet who had become a turtle, Denise felt that the turtle had been diminished, demoted from a sensitive human, just as she herself has been diminished in her work life. When Denise awoke, she was still crying. What if she was unable to recapture her own more sensitive side? What if her previous handling of her life couldn't be reversed and that spirited turtle was gone forever?

Denise's dream had almost immediate fallout. The dream helped her to face her situation in a way she couldn't deny or minimize. The turtle's distress and her painful loss of him prompted her to put an end to the troubling loss of meaning she had been experiencing in her work. Relying on savings, she quit her job and began the task of figuring out how to bring her life into balance again. In so viscerally portraying her dilemma, her dream gave her the push she needed to make a major life change.

Denise has now been away from her old job for a couple of months. She doesn't know if she will return to her old line of work in a new way, or if a new line of work will emerge over time. As the time away from her old job increases, she feels lighter, but is anxious about the future. She's in that uncomfortable phase of transition when the old has been stripped away but the new hasn't yet emerged. When she's tempted to retreat to her old job, she uses her dream as a touchstone and remembers the distress she felt before she quit. In this sense, her dream both initiated a major change and is helping her to stay the course as she navigates an important transition.

Denise's dream is a new one and she doesn't yet know where it will lead. The next big dream, from Bob Quinn of Portland, Oregon, was dreamed many years ago. He has had years to work on the meaning of his dream and to understand the dream's role in his professional and personal development.

A Dream That Shaped His Work

Bob Quinn is an acupuncturist and herbalist. A lifelong dreamer, he has had several big dreams. At the time he had this particular dream, Bob was a part-owner of an herb company and had a small practice as an acupuncturist in Portland. Although he had earned a masters degree in acupuncture, he was uncertain as a practitioner. His school had taught Chinese acupuncture, with which he didn't resonate, and there was no support in Portland for the gentler Japanese acupuncture that attracted him more. At the time of his dream, Bob had taken a few introductory courses in Japanese acupuncture and was trying out that approach with a few patients, but he felt depleted and at a loss about his future as a healer.

Bob's big dream included the wise person often present in a big dream. She offered him direction about his future as a practitioner.

> *I am handed a flyer by my mother. It is an advertisement for an acupuncture clinic. At the bottom is a website address, then the scene switches and I am suddenly in the clinic in question. It is in New York State near the northern edge of the Adirondack State Park, not far from the Canadian border. In the clinic I encounter a young female Chinese Medicine practitioner who has amazing treatment skills. Her name is Mead. At one point she hands me a ball of twine to unravel, and I am all thumbs with it. She combines Japanese Meridian Therapy (a style of acupuncture), Sotai (a Japanese style of neuromuscular reeducation), Yin-Yang Channel Balancing (another Japanese style of acupuncture), and Trager bodywork, a style developed by the late Milton Trager, MD. All of these ways of working with patients are exceedingly gentle.*

Bob's dream self could see that Mead was an accomplished healer, far beyond him in her skills. When she handed him the ball of twine and he fumbled it, he was embarrassed. It was obvious that he had a long path ahead to develop the skills she represented.

When Bob awoke, he felt that his dream clearly supported the Japanese work he wanted to offer in his practice. The three types of Japanese work Mead integrated were ones he had begun to study. The Trager work was a surprise. He didn't know anything about it. He had a sense that if he followed Mead's lead, the path would be sweet, just as her name suggested.

The affirmation Bob felt in this dream spurred major life changes. He sold his condo and his share of the herb company and set off on an open-ended journey to see where this dream would lead him. This leap into the unknown was frightening but he knew he couldn't follow the wisdom of his dream if he stayed in Portland. He worked at the herb company because he didn't have faith in himself as a healer and there were no teachers in Portland to instruct him.

Bob's journey proved to be a thirteen-month "walkabout," during which he stayed with different friends and continued to pay close attention to his dreams. In the course of his journey, he met important teachers in two of the traditions suggested in his dream. One of these teachers would become a mentor with whom he worked over several summers. He also found a woman who began to teach him Trager work in exchange for acupuncture sessions.

After thirteen months, with only $200 left to his name, Bob returned to Portland where he began to develop the synthesis of styles that were presented in his dream. Having followed the wisdom of his dream and having met the mentors he needed, he was more confident in his own path, and things fell into place for him. A stream of new patients arrived in his treatment room. He also received a full scholarship to his old acupuncture school where he developed Japanese acupuncture styles while working on his doctorate.

The path of gentle acupuncture not only brought these outer gifts, it was also a path of spiritual development. Bob says that he has always had a quick, impatient mind. The gentle acupuncture forced him to slow down and become more present—to think with his hands rather than his mind. His work, as supported by his dream, resulted in spiritual and professional refinement.

Two Red Chests

Freud famously said, "Love and work are the cornerstones of our humanity." In Jung's paired dreams about his course of study, in

Denise's turtle dream, and in Bob's dream of meeting a dream-time healer, we see the unconscious addressing the cornerstone of work. In the next two dreams, we see the unconscious addressing love, specifically the archetypal gateway of marriage.

My own dream, "Red Chests," came to me a few weeks before I met my husband. This dream prepared me for the sea change of marriage. I was in my forties when I had the dream and had been single for almost fifteen years after an early marriage ended badly. I wanted an enduring partnership but had emotional baggage: guilt about how I had handled my first marriage, and mistrust of closeness from difficulties in my early life. The shorter relationships I was in during those fifteen years were discouraging and increased my reservations about marriage.

A few weeks before I met my husband, I had a dream set in Canada where my family has had a summer home for over a hundred years. When my parents were alive, they often stayed in a room in our house that had side-by-side crimson chests painted with blue and yellow hearts. In waking life, my parents each used one of these chests and placed personal items on the surface of the chest. My mother's chest had lotions and her current needlepoint project. My father's had his billfold, a thick novel, and the spare change he carried in his pocket. Although I had noticed these chests over the years, they hadn't meant much to me. Here is "Red Chests," the dream that prepared me to meet my husband.

> *I'm in Canada and meet up with William, a distant cousin whom I have always been attracted to. The sexual and emotional energy between us is intense and he asks me if I want to marry him. Although I am strongly tempted, I also am reluctant, due to my emotional baggage about marriage. As I stand talking to him, I flash on the red chests in my parents' room. In my mind's eyes, they are pulsing with energy and are*

surrounded by a nimbus of light. They seem alive and remind me of two hearts, separate, but standing side by side. I am deeply touched by my vision of those pulsating chests, how they stand beside each other, year after year. I begin to weep and say to William that, yes, I will marry him.

When I awoke from this dream, I was still crying. The archetypal power of marriage had been projected onto those two chests, and in experiencing them deeply, I felt the value of standing beside another no matter what comes. I saw that while my parents' marriage had been flawed, they had stood like those chests, side to side, for over fifty years. I was moved by what I now understood and my view of marriage shifted. I didn't marry my distant cousin but my dream prepared me to meet Roger, my future husband, several weeks later.

It's important to add that this big dream didn't appear in a vacuum. I had been working on my obstacles to long-term commitment for several years. I had gone to therapy to explore my emotional issues. I also had taken a break from intimate relationships for several years so that I could reset the patterns I was bringing into my relationships. My waking self had done everything possible to ready myself for a more enduring relationship, and through my dream, my unconscious provided a powerful image that furthered my readiness. The result of that collaboration is a marriage I cherish, now in its twenty-fifth year.

A Bride in her Canoe

John Williams, a psychotherapist and artist who lives in Arizona, also had a dream that helped him to move toward marriage. During the months leading up to his marriage, John experienced a good deal of wordless anxiety about this commitment. Although he loved his partner Leona, he was filled with worries and self-doubts and was having trouble sleeping. The peaceful quality and power of his dream provided a positive confirmation of John and Leona's plan to marry and was an antidote to the anxiety he had been feeling.

As John says of his dream, "The images in the dream foretold that the marriage was based on a solid foundation with the blessings of the gods and the animals."

> *Leona or an Indian princess is wearing a cloth headdress. She is floating by, silently, in a canoe accompanied by a procession of swimming animals—deer, ducks, snakes, bears, fish. As the procession passes by me, the woman in the canoe throws a golden key into the water behind her canoe. A golden light shines up from the water where the key dropped.*

John's dream was packed with archetypal and animal imagery, which is so often an important part of our big dreams. The woman in the canoe, in her ceremonial headdress, was perhaps Leona, perhaps a princess. The blurring between the everyday woman and a princess placed her in a transpersonal realm beyond our everyday experience.

Accompanying the canoe was a breathtaking collection of animals. This rich diversity suggested that many benevolent forces were supporting the bride as she traveled in her canoe. The diversity also suggested that many kinds of positive energies existed in the connection between John and Leona.

A final archetypal element, familiar in fairy tales, was the gold key the princess threw into the water. The key was perhaps connected to the initiation of marriage and the unlocking of that important archetypal experience. After the princess threw the key into the water, it became a golden light. Perhaps marriage to this princess would offer warmth and guidance to the waters of John's psyche.

It's important to note John's way of working with his dreams in general and with this one in particular. Although he has a good understanding of mythology and psychology, he doesn't tend to intellectualize about the meaning of his dreams. He engages with them in silence and allows the power of the images to deepen him. Sometimes, as with this dream, he creates art inspired by a dream's imagery. In the case of his marriage dream, he created a clay relief of the dream's images that he exhibited during his marriage ceremony. The presence of these images helped to bring the power of his dream to his marriage day and to sanctify it.

Since John's marriage to Leona fifteen years ago, a vision of the canoe has occasionally reemerged, although he now sees both himself and Leona traveling in it. This soothing image has appeared particularly in times of transition or change. The image of the gold key has never returned. Instead, there is a gold light in the water that they together follow.

They Stay With Us

In this chapter, we've seen the powerful effects of the big, unforgettable dreams that meet us at the gates of a new life cycle. Sometimes these dreams further something we consciously have hoped for and sometimes these dreams stun us, pushing us in unanticipated directions.

The imagery of these dreams often stays with us for the rest of our lives, because of the beauty and power of the images and because sea changes are connected with that imagery. Our big dreams become an important part of our life story. As "life begets dream begets life begets dream," our unique destiny emerges.

Explorations

- Have you ever experienced a big dream? You will recognize it by the impact it had on you in the dream itself and in your life afterwards. If it was a big dream, you'll know it.
- If you have a big dream, practice extra humility. A big dream may take years to comprehend fully. As your understanding of your life path deepens over time and as the changes initiated by your dream occur, you will better understand the multiple meanings of the dream.
- When you have a big dream, think of it as a touchstone you can use to ground yourself as the changes initiated by your dream occur. The dream will help you to accept the risks involved in making changes.
- Trust your dream. Big dreams upset the status quo and we often feel anxious as well as excited by them. Remember the stories in this chapter and how big dreams are part of a new phase of development. Trust the changes that may be part of taking the next step in your development.
- Find a friend, a guide, or a dream group where you can share the impact of your dream. It's good to have company as we navigate the changes following a big dream.

Chapter Six

Stepping Stones

Our big dreams are dramatic dreamtime experiences that catapult us into a different phase of life. They are gateways to new cycles in our unique destiny. Many of our dreams are less impactful. They respond to the small daily challenges and imbalances that are part of every phase of life. Many of our dreams are like stepping stones that provide reflection and guidance as we make our way, step by small step, dream by small dream, through life.

Just as any chapter of our outer life has persistent themes and challenges, so our dream life has its own themes that clarify and balance our conscious attitudes during that period. Some of our stepping-stone dreams are vivid and we remember them. Others are less memorable. If we re-read them later in our dreams journal, we have no recollection of them.

In their book *Dreams, A Portal to the Source*, Edward Whitmont and Sylvia Perrera wrote about what they call *dream series* and what I think of as stepping-stone dreams:

> Until now, we have been dealing with single dreams. However, there is a continuity, as we might almost say, an extended story, as dreams unfold sequentially, as part of a steadily evolving series. They tend to tell a

> running narrative, which feeds the conscious ego the kind of information it requires and is able to assimilate, given its particular position in the developmental process. As consciousness takes in and responds to the dream's messages, the dreams again respond to the newly gained positions of consciousness; thus a dialectical play develops.[39]

This dialectical play is the living loop described in Chapter Two. As we absorb a dream's perspectives, we adjust our attitudes and actions based on the dream. Our adjusted attitudes and actions have their own limitations, and new dreams then offer their perspectives on those. During any given stage of development, our outer lives and our dream lives weave together in service of meeting the challenges of life.

The Baby Book

In the course of my life, I've had many sequences of stepping-stone dreams. One such sequence of dreams accompanied the creation of this book. As noted in the introduction, my dream "Looking for a Book to Write" provided the first inkling that I might write a book about how dreams help us to create our lives. A few months into writing the book, I had the dream, "Not Getting the Task Done," described in Chapter One. That dream presented the different parts of me that were derailing the book project: an inner teenager who didn't want the responsibility, an adult who had lost focus, and a punk who was undermining my confidence with negative messages.

After "Not Getting the Job Done," I settled into collecting dreams and writing up dream stories. Six months later, I had two dreams showing that the time of equivocation was long gone. The theme of birth and babies in these dreams reflected how deeply committed I was to birthing this book. I titled the first one "The Baby Book."

> *I'm walking through rough terrain with a baby clinging to my body. I'm trying to help the baby get strong enough so that it can lie in the sun free of my body and soak up sunlight. I don't want it to grow up, just to have enough independence that it can lie in the sun and maybe be tended by other people occasionally. However, this baby isn't that far along. It's tiny and stuck to my body. A couple of times its head comes off, like a doll's head, and I have to adjust it, to get it set on straight. I so want this baby to be a bit more independent, but it must cling to me to survive.*

When I had this dream, I was deeply engaged, but also feeling isolated. I yearned to share my writing with other people. However, I had only written segments of several chapters. As much as I wanted to break out of my isolation, the book didn't feel ready to be reviewed by an editor or colleagues. My book, like the baby in the dream, was too immature to be separated from me and to lie in the clarity of the day. The baby still needed to be connected exclusively to me. This dream clearly presented where I was in the process, and helped me to accept the isolation I felt.

The image of the head coming off and needing to be adjusted amused me. I recognized my earlier struggles to find the right voice and tone for this book. Once I wrote a whole chapter that was so stilted and boring that I had to tear up every page of the chapter. The head came off the baby, and I had to reset it.

I called a second dream, that I had shortly thereafter, "A Pregnant Older Woman."

> *I'm searching for friends or a community that I can't find. I see an older woman who reminds me of a poet I know in Oregon.*

> *At one point, I see this woman fold herself carefully into a hole so that she is completely camouflaged. I notice that she is pregnant. I then see the father of her baby. He's an absolutely gorgeous being, not from this world at all. Looks around 30.*

The poet in this dream is someone my age with a similar background and a similar love of poetry. It was clear that she represented me in the dream. Having a surrogate provided a perspective I wouldn't have had if my dream self had been pregnant. As I watched the pregnant poet from a distance, I could see her pregnancy was hidden from the world. This resonated with how my book and my labors were hidden from the world.

This imagery was also meaningful to me because this older woman was being held in the earth like a fetus, even as she was carrying her own child. This squared with my experience that that I was birthing a book, but that the book was also birthing me.

In spite of having written several other books, I had never engaged in a project that lasted more than a year and I had had many kinds of assistance in my earlier projects. When I wrote a dissertation, I had the support of teachers and colleagues in my school program. When I wrote a mass-market paperback many years ago, I was very fortunate to have a book packager, an editor, a publisher, and a hefty advance to fund the project. This current project was totally dependent on my own belief in the project and on my own stamina. My isolation with the project demanded new levels of patience and trust—qualities that didn't always come easily to me.

The choice of this particular poet to represent me offered comfort. I know her as an intelligent person with a quirky, original intellect. Having her represent me suggested that maybe my own work would have its own authenticity and originality.

The other character in my dream was the beautiful father of the baby, someone from another realm. He was gorgeous.

This too reflected the book. Both the project itself and all of the dreams in this book originated in the unconscious, a place of otherworldly beauty and power. A laboring older woman (me) and a beautiful otherworldly presence (the unconscious) were the parents of the project.

While dreams continued to accompany me during the writing of this book, Rick Schooley, an artist from San Rafael, California, had a sequence of three dreams during a time of rapid growth in his life. Rick's dreams reflect the considerable effort required to birth a new self.

Rick's Dreams of Liberation

From age eighteen through his early thirties, Rick was engaged in a slow and often arduous process of healing from the dysfunctions of his childhood. He participated in both individual and group therapies to learn to take better care of himself and to build a stronger sense of self.

In his early thirties, Rick took on the challenge of working twelves12 Step programs for alcohol and gambling. Once clean and sober, he felt like "a veil had been lifted" and that he was able to see himself and his life more clearly. Even his senses felt sharper. He remembers an experience of watching the wind blowing through trees. He was awed by this simple beauty and realized that he hadn't seen the world this clearly since he was fifteen years old.

This period of early recovery was a time of expansion and liberation for Rick. Freed from addictions, he was better able to apply what he had learned in his earlier therapies. During this time, he began an important relationship with a woman. Being sober allowed him to be present in a close relationship in a new way. He also became part of a professional acting workshop and a dream group. These experiences opened him to new parts of himself and new ways of being with others.

The three dreams that follow are dreams that Rick had during this period of expansion. Although he had these dreams many years ago, they have stayed with him. They provided powerful reflection on the demanding transformation he was undergoing at that time. This is the first dream:

> *There is a spinning human whom I feel is me. I'm covered in armor plates and with each spin, more armor falls off. This process continues for four or five seconds. Then I wake up.*

Rick's experience at this time was of becoming vulnerable in many new ways. The armor, spinning off in layers, felt to him like old defenses—alcohol, gambling, and ways he had become distanced from himself and the world—dropping away. This dream was an important validation both of his recovery from addictions and of the new activities in his outer life. Layer by layer, he was becoming more open to life.

In this dream, the main character was spinning. Although this was an exciting period in his life, Rick was experiencing many things for the first time without the protection of addiction. His life was dizzying and overwhelming as well as exciting and affirming. The dream reflected the effort and increased vulnerability of this time.

Rick's second dream, about pulling metal from his mouth, continued the theme of liberation from cold, hard metal that had been confining him.

> *I don't know where I am, but I'm pulling metal braces and materials out of my mouth, like from an orthodontist. The dream ends as I am pulling out more and more of it.*

The first dream presented a spinning man whom Rick felt was himself. There was a distance between Rick's observing self and the spinning man. In the second dream, there was no separation. Rick's dream self was actively and intentionally pulling metal from his mouth. Rick wasn't spinning. He was hard at work at a difficult task.

Rick related the dream to re-learning to speak at this point in his recovery. As a young boy in sports, he sometimes spoke in a bullying way to other boys. As an adolescent on the streets of San Francisco, he had picked up the habit of using slang and profanity. When he became sober, he heard himself as if for the first time and realized that he wanted to change how he communicated. To do that, he had to pull out all the old habits and begin to use language more consciously.

Rick's association to the metal in his mouth was wearing braces as a child. The metal strap and metal retainer he wore at night had been constricting and sometimes slapped against his face. Like his retainer, his old patterns of speech had been painful and Rick was determined to change them. In his acting, his dream group, and his new relationship, he created the opportunity to use language in a way more attuned to his own feelings and to those of other people.

In Rick's final remembered dream from this period, he met the Loch Ness Monster.

> *I'm fishing from a small boat. My fishing pole starts bending and I can tell it's something big. A few seconds later, I pull it out, and discover much to my surprise that it's the Loch Ness Monster. It doesn't frighten me. The dream shifts and the Loch Ness Monster is climbing onto the shore. It looks very tired from the whole ordeal. Then the dream ends.*

In his dream, Rick wasn't frightened by the monster. In fact, he felt compassion for a creature so exhausted from being pulled up from the depths. Rick related the monster to the hidden spirit in himself. He noted that the Loch Ness Monster appears and disappears, and that it is difficult to get a consistent view of it. Similarly, it can be difficult to hold a clear and consistent view of the spirit within our self.

The dream spoke to Rick's long journey to strip away defenses and to remake himself as a more receptive human being. Perhaps at one point long ago, his hidden self had seemed frightening and monstrous to him, as unconscious aspects of our self can feel alien and threatening. If his hidden spirit had ever been threatening, those days were long gone. Rick now felt only compassion for this creature.

An additional association of Rick's was the pain that sea creatures must have felt as they transformed from sea to land animals. In Rick's dream, the monster was making that transformation. He had suffered a lot to get there, just as Rick had suffered as he brought hidden parts of himself into consciousness.

Rick's dreams were part of building a new foundation for himself, of remaking his life in a more authentic way. His hard work eventually resulted in his success as an artist—creating hundreds of paintings of the natural world and sharing his pictures with others.

Sister Mary Returns to the Motherhouse

Like Rick, Sister Mary, a Roman Catholic nun, had a series of important stepping-stone dreams during a period of major transition. She had close to a hundred dreams in the fifteen months leading up to her retirement from a California high school and her return to her motherhouse in the Midwest. In the process of leaving, she had to say goodbye to people she loved and to parts of herself she had valued for many decades.

When she was a young girl, Sister Mary first experienced her calling to become a religious. As she knelt in front of a statue of Our Lady of Sorrows in her midwestern parish, she felt that she would like to spend her life making people happy. After graduating from high school, she followed up on this early calling when she entered a Roman Catholic order.

Sister Mary's college education in biology and elementary education prepared her for her career as a biology teacher. After teaching in the Mmidwest, she relocated to a Catholic high school in California. During her long service at this school, Sister Mary participated in many aspects of school life, first as a teacher and later as a school counselor. She taught biological sciences to generations of students. Her hands-on approach included participation in a community garden, trips to beaches to learn about the maritime ecosystem, and the collection of local shells and flora. Hundreds of students remembered the inspirational quotes that appeared on the blackboard every day. Later Sister Mary became a Licensed Marriage and Family Therapist and offered emotional support to struggling students and their families.

Sister Mary also participated in school retreats, trips to the United Nations, campus sports, and the various big events of community life. As time passed, her students became parents who sent their own children to the school. Over the years, she became close to many families and treasured her connection to them.

In her late seventies, Sister Mary received another call, this time to return to her motherhouse in the Mmidwest. As with the first calling when she was a child, this call came from within. Many of the sisters in her order were sick and dying, and she felt guided to help them, though she felt intimidated by the prospect.

During the months of her transition, Mary's dreams accompanied her through complicated territory. Some themes, like loss, uncertainty, and the hard work of transitioning, appeared many times. The dreams that follow provide a clear sense of how our dreams reflect and guide us through important transitions.

One of Sister Mary's first stepping-stone dreams occurred in June of 2017, shortly after she decided to move back to the motherhouse.

> *I travel by car with Susan, my principal, and someone I don't know to a Los Angeles convent for a celebration. Susan leaves her things in the car—a potluck dish and her purse—but I take my billfold and coin purse in and immediately worry about carrying them. I'm warmly greeted by the Sisters. People are visiting and moving around while waiting for Mass to begin. I lose my billfold almost immediately. It doesn't have much of value in it but nonetheless it is nowhere and probably will never be seen again. As Mass begins, the chapel is packed and I'm in the back, not knowing where my two travel companions are seated. My pew is a little offset. Where will I kneel?*

In this dream, Sister Mary traveled with the principal of her school to a place where a religious celebration was occurring, a clear parallel to her journey from her school life to a new life in the motherhouse. Sister Mary was warmly greeted by the Sisters, as she expected to be when she returned to the midwest. However, in the course of the dream, she lost many things. She lost her billfold, perhaps symbolic of her identity as a wage earner and her independence in managing her money. She lost connection with her principal and the other woman she traveled with, a preview of the loss of important relationships as she moved away from the school. Finally, she didn't know where to kneel. She knew she needed to kneel but her place was not yet determined. Sister Mary appropriately called this dream, "Loss and Uncertainty."

A fragment of another dream from the same period also reflected threat.

I'm in a house and the river outside is rising. It overcomes the house, roaring around on either side of it. I think of going out the back door, but the water is there too. I say to the person I'm with, "I'm done. Say your prayers. We are going to die."

Often in our dreams, a house represents the state of our personality at that moment in time. In this dream, Sister Mary and her house were endangered by a roaring river, the strong conscious and unconscious emotions that were coursing through her. Her fear that she would not be able to survive this transition was palpable.

In the fall of 2017, Sister Mary began the process of dismantling her physical life in California. She sorted through forty years of collected belongings, giving away her camping gear, her succulents, and many photographs she had taken. Giving the right things to the right people made this process sweeter. She also visited her motherhouse and began to make specific plans about her life once she returned there. The relative ease of this period was reflected in her dream called "Smooth Waters and Tangling Weeds."

I'm on a body of water that's covered by a plastic-like coating. I slither over it. It undulates and shines quietly, sometimes like a rainbow. Someone else I don't see or recognize is also there behind me.

A second time I'm crossing the large lake again as before. This time I reach an inlet where the coating ends and there is water in the tongue-like inlet. I swim a bit and then stand up. My legs get tangled in the water's weeds. I think the unknown someone helps me get untangled. The scene is tactile, not scary.

Unlike the water in her earlier river dream, the water in this dream was smooth and calm. In fact, it was covered by a plastic-like coating which suggested a kind of separation from her deeper emotions.

When her dream self reached an inlet of open water beyond the plastic coating, her legs became tangled in weeds and her dream self had to untangle them. However, she had unseen help and didn't find the situation frightening. The parallel with disengaging from her possession and commitments was clear, but at this moment, she was not frightened by her situation.

The relative calm of the fall faded as winter approached and Sister Mary prepared to tell colleagues and friends that she would be leaving at the end of the school year. Two short dreams reflected the hard work and disorientation of saying goodbye.

> "Slippery Shoreline"
> *I'm on the shoreline of the lake where my family went when I was a child. I try to get up on land but the bank is too sandy and I can't get a foothold and keep sliding back down. Finally, I move left and find a lower bank to climb up.*

> "Derailment!"
> *I'm in a train yard and cars are moving all around me, countless cars! Finally, some derail.*

These dreams clearly reflected the backsliding and derailment Mary was feeling as she took her life apart. Sister Mary had a strong vision of the rightness of her move and a good practical sense of how to organize the many parts of it. It was sometimes harder for her to stay in touch with the pain of her situation. Dreams like these kept her in touch with the feelings connected to this transition.

In the spring of 2018, Sister Mary continued to gently and consciously detach from her life in California and to create the beautiful ending that was important to her. A powerful dream that spring affirmed the goodness of her life's work.

I'm touring an Art Gallery and see several interesting works of art. I come upon a stunning one. It's quite large, maybe 5 ft. tall by 3 ft. wide. In the art piece on the bottom left is a figure in brown. Behind the figure and above it is a group of people also in brown. No one has features but the bottom left figure seems to have influenced the group in some positive way. The arm belonging to the lower left figure is extending out toward the group and is highlighted, clothed or robed. The artwork is rich, thick brown with yellow accents and framed in gold. Beautiful, simple, strong. The piece is monk-like but not really. It speaks of the earth— simplicity, honesty, richness, life-giving.

At first, this dream was mysterious to Sister Mary. Her association that works of art are completed things enabled her to see that the dream was about a beloved career, a beautiful work of art, that was now complete. As she related to the picture as a representation of her work, the meaning of the dream opened. She saw herself as the figure in the lower left corner, a person who had leant a helping hand to the rows of faceless figures. That these figures were brown made sense to her since her work had been to connect students to the earth and to help many generations of students "to become earthy." This dream validated the beauty of her career, providing a reflection she needed in order to let go and move on in a graceful manner.

Another dream from the early summer also presented her with a reflection of the value of her life. She called this dream, "Unimagined Wealth."

I walk up away from my childhood home for an unknown reason. The street has changed since childhood! I hesitate then go over a dirt embankment and scramble over a hedge-like rise to get onto the parking lot. The once familiar stores are gone.

I take a walk and find myself on a street lined on both sides with very beautiful old banks. At the street's end, I turn the corner and there is a store full of gorgeous lladros! Huge, even statue-sized ones!

There are lots of folks of all sorts walking the street. I turn another corner past a bus stop, looking for street signs to find my way home. I am completely lost in totally unfamiliar territory.

This dream offered a picture of her life journey. She had left home and after a small climb, found herself on a street lined with beautiful banks. Her life of service had been filled with riches like those in the beautiful banks. The lladros, the finest porcelain statues, were perhaps similar to the painting in her earlier dream—representations of the artistry of her life. The many celebrations of Sister Mary's life that spring had helped to solidify the riches that the dream reflected to her.

At the end of the dream, Sister Mary turned a corner, looking for her way home, and found herself in unknown territory. In her outer life, she had said her goodbyes to California and made the necessary arrangements for returning to the motherhouse. She had turned a corner and was now in the unknown, looking for her new home.

One of Sister Mary's final dreams before her move was a dream she called "My New Friends." This dream, not surprisingly, presented the archetypal image of the snake.

I'm on an undulating netted platform that then solidifies. It is light green. There are two huge snakes there. One is moving toward me. The snake is scary, but not seemingly threatening. It comes close up to me (nose to nose) but does not communicate. It acts like it means business.

The second snake tries to climb up the wall to my left toward what appears to be a crucifix. It falls.

Then a third snake appears and wraps itself around my neck, but is furry and warm. It seems to have like a fur collar. I am not frightened but not thrilled either.

I sense there is something really important going on here.

The snake, which molts its skin, is one of the major cross-cultural symbols of transformation and rebirth. It's the symbol for the kundalini energy that moves up the spine from the lower centers to higher centers, and represents the transmutation of energy to a higher spiritual vibration. When we have snake dreams, we know that we are in the midst of a powerful, spiritual transformation.

Sister Mary's dream presented not one but three snakes. The first snake was scary but not threatening. The power of her transition couldn't be minimized, but her transition wasn't threatening to destroy her, as had been the case in her early river dream. The second snake in Mary's dream headed up a wall toward a crucifix but fell. After years of studying many different forms of psychology and spirituality, Sister Mary was returning to the motherhouse. That the second snake fell away from the crucifix suggested that the integration with a more traditional Christianity at the motherhouse might hold challenges in the future. The final snake in Sister Mary's dream wrapped itself around her neck. It was warm and furry, comforting, but she was wary, not making the mistake of considering the powerful snake a pet.

This dream left no doubt—Sister Mary was not through her transformation. Much still awaited her. Her return to the motherhouse was not a retirement from life, but rather part of a spiritual reorganization that would reshape her relationship to herself and the world.

My book dreams, Rick's dreams of rebuilding himself, and Sister Mary's transition dreams are examples of dreams that guide us through a particular cycle of life. If we pay attention, a sequence of dreams emerges that reflects different aspects of our life passage. Our dreams and our waking lives weave together, helping our destinies to unfold.

Explorations

- Consider the themes and challenges that are part of the life passage you're currently in. What new parts of you are trying to emerge? How are you being challenged to grow your current attitudes and limitations?

- When you have a dream, write it down in your dream journal and use your dream tools to open the meaning of your dream Pay close attention to how your dream relates to the current unfolding of your life. What kind of feedback are you receiving on your waking self's attitudes, actions, and challenges?

- What themes are recurring in your dreams during this cycle in your life? Are you having any any big dreams or repeating dreams?

- Notice the weave between your waking and dream lives, as you are led forward, dream by dream.

Chapter Seven

The Ones That Come Again and Again

From our earliest dreams onward, our unconscious helps us to manifest our unique destinies. Big dreams, with their powerful archetypal imagery, meet us at the gates of major change and help us to pass through those gates. Stepping-stone dreams lead us, step by step, dream by dream, through a transition or life passage. Our recurring dreams, the ones that repeat, have another function in our development. Time and again, they focus our attention on an unresolved issue or experience. This experience may be a devastating trauma, an ongoing imbalance in our life, or a loss or failure we haven't fully accepted. The unresolved experience is like a psychic knot that needs to be untied, and until we untie it, a dream may appear many times as our unconscious attempts to bring our attention to the problem.

In *Working with Dreams*, Montague Ullman and Nancy Zimmerman wrote about this function of our dream life:

> All of us have emotional residues from our past that we haven't quite disposed of: particular areas of vulnerability that get bruised from time to time in the

> course of our lives. When this happens, we often have a dream which depicts the problem and shows where we are in relation to it. If we fail to make progress in this particular area that is giving us trouble, we are apt to encounter the same problem in in our lives and to dream about it in the same way.[40]

It's easy to become frustrated or irritated with recurring dreams. Just as we can become frustrated with the tenacity of some of our waking challenges, we also can become frustrated with the insistence of these dreams. I remember a client who, over the years, had scores of dreams about his wallet being stolen. Any time he felt powerless or made a poor decision in his waking life, his wallet was stolen in the dream world. One night, after decades of these dreams, he stood up in his dream and yelled, "No more. I don't want any more wallet dreams."

While I understood my client's frustration, I have another feeling about recurring dreams. I feel comforted by the tenacity of the unconscious. Like an insistent mother, our unconscious never gives up on us and continues to repeat its perspective until we make the needed adjustment in our inner or outer life.

Some recurring dreams are recognizable both to frequent dreamers and to people who rarely dream. These dreams, expressing our universally shared vulnerability, indicate that we feel overwhelmed and short of the resources we need. Some commonly shared recurring dreams include free-falling, being trapped in an out-of-control automobile, being chased, and appearing naked in public. These dreams can be generic with not much individualized detail, or can contain individualized symbolism and details that are meaningful to us.

Susan's Intruder

When people have experienced devastating trauma, they often repress their memory of some or all of that trauma in order to survive. Often that repressed trauma will be revealed in recurring dreams that attempt to bring the painful experience to conscious awareness. This was the case with Susan Ralston, a retired chemistry professor from Florida. Susan was sexually abused at age five and dreamed about a frightening intruder for decades afterward.

When Susan was in graduate school, she had an abusive sexual experience that activated her early abuse. During this experience, Susan had a strong waking vision of a male torso, once muscular, now gone to fat. This torso was different from the long narrow torso of the young man forcing himself on her. The image of this torso haunted Susan for weeks afterwards and was accompanied by unbearable anxiety. She had difficulty sleeping and when she did sleep, she had disturbing dreams of an intruder breaking into her home as she slept.

One night during this period of unbearable anxiety, Susan had a dissociative experience where her consciousness hovered on the ceiling of the bathroom, staring down at her body in the tub. The morning after this experience, she poured sleeping pills into a pile and began swallowing them. Fortunately, she came to her senses and ran from her apartment to find her roommate. With her roommate's help Susan was hospitalized, and soon after, she began the psychotherapy that started her on the path to recovery.

After this period of acute distress, Susan was in years of therapy where she received help with depression and food issues. From time to time, her early abuse emerged, but her therapy focused mostly on struggles in her current life. A strong and determined individual, Susan was able to channel her anger at her abuse into support of women's rights at her university in Florida.

Although Susan's attention was focused on her adult life rather than on her early trauma, her intruder dreams continued. The following dream is a typical one:

> *I'm in bed sleeping. A man with a knife is hidden in the shadows and is sneaking up the back stairs toward my room. I hear him coming and am terrified. Although I want to hide, I'm paralyzed, unable to move. I hear his footsteps coming closer and closer, and awaken in a panic.*

Many years later, Susan retired from her career and moved to a beach town in Florida. Soon after her retirement, she had the following dream, which initiated a new round of therapy:

> *In the first part of the dream, I watch a five-year-old girl with curly blond hair being terrorized by a huge extraterrestrial worm.*
>
> *In the next part of the dream, I'm an adult and am trying to contain the worm by wrapping foil around it. However, I'm losing the battle. Parts of the worm are breaking out from the wrapping. I feel anxious that I can't keep that worm wrapped up.*

A practiced dreamworker, Susan understood that a huge extraterrestrial worm attacking a five-year-old was an image of the sexual assault she suffered as a child. She knew that her adult self's failure to keep the worm "under wraps" meant that she needed to make another dive into what happened to her as a child. Susan was discouraged that after years of therapy, she still had more psychological work to do. Her heightened anxiety, however, made it clear that she had to face the intruder who had been lurking in her dreams for decades.

During Susan's late-in-life therapy, she had the time and the strength to identify her abuser. As fragments of memory from her childhood emerged, it became clear that her intruder dreams were not metaphorical. Her abuser had been an actual intruder in her home.

When Susan was five and blond, like the little girl in her dream, she was laid up in bed for many weeks. In addition to recuperating from a tonsillectomy, she had a bad case of chicken pox. While Susan was bedridden, a stranger lived in her home. A friend of a distant cousin, he stayed with her family for a few months while he received medical treatment at a local hospital. In May and June, Susan spent hours alone and sick in her room on the second floor of her house, while this stranger spent his days in the bedroom next to hers. Her mother spent most of her time on the first floor in another part of the house, doing household tasks.

As Susan pieced together what happened to her, the image of the flabby torso returned, bringing with it high levels of anxiety. As Susan considered the different men in her childhood, she realized that none of them had a chest like the one that haunted her. However, the flabby chest could have been that of the man who stayed with her family.

Some corroboration came from her brother, who remembered some disturbing things about this guest's sexual boundaries. Another important piece of corroboration was that Susan's suicide attempt and hospitalization as a young adult occurred during May and June, the same months she had been bedridden with a stranger in the next room. Susan may have forgotten her early trauma, but her unconscious clearly remembered who her abuser was and when the abuse occurred.

For decades, Susan's unconscious sent dreams that reminded her of her unresolved abuse. When she had the time and the inner strength to investigate her early abuse in more depth, her dreams alerted her that she had another piece of psychological work to do. In this late-in-life investigation, she was able to at last identify the man who was most likely her abuser and the stalker who had haunted her dreams.

Kidnapped

While Susan's recurring dreams were related to a trauma, my most memorable recurring dream was connected to an impasse in my life. They were dreams that brought attention to a knot that needed to be unraveled in the early years of my marriage.

At the time of these dreams, I was living in the San Francisco Bay Area and my life was flourishing. A late bloomer, I was enjoying my full psychotherapy practice. In addition, I was teaching psychology classes at a local graduate school and supervising several interns. Because success came late to me, I treasured the riches in my professional life and never took them for granted. In addition to professional successes, I had many friends I loved. Some friendships went back decades and offered the comfort shared by people who know each other well. Other friendships were new and exciting. My life was rich and fertile, the best it had ever been.

A few years into this new contentment, I met my husband who had lived in the Bay Area for a decade and was ready to move away. Although we had different ideas about where to live, we married and carried our differing needs, as well as our love for each other, into our marriage. This began several years of conflict. I cared deeply for my husband and wanted him to have the life he wanted. I also wanted to enjoy the life I had worked hard to establish.

During the years of this conflict, my husband and I looked at many places to move. We developed a pattern of checking out a new location and then I would back out and refuse to leave the Bay Area. Accompanying my abortive attempts to move were dozens of dreams about being kidnapped. My dream self could be man, woman, or child. The dream could take place in the present or in a different historical period. The only thing that remained constant was that I was snatched away from my life and was never rescued. Here is a typical dream from that period:

> *I'm a 12-year-old boy who has been kidnapped by gypsies. I'm tied up and scared, but am also scheming inside my head about ways to escape. I can't see how that will happen, but I haven't given up hope.*

This dream had the usual elements of my recurring dreams: I had been kidnapped and felt helpless. In this dream, I hadn't given up hope, but I was unable to think my way out of the situation. When I considered this dream, I was interested that I had been kidnapped by gypsies. I associated gypsies with an itinerant lifestyle and in my waking life, I felt I was being asked to pull up roots and live like a gypsy.

I was also interested that my dream self was a twelve-year-old boy. I wondered if a masculine, assertive part of myself had been wounded at that age. Looking back, I remembered that at twelve, I transferred from public school to a private girls' school. This adjustment had been difficult. I was behind academically and had to make a place for myself socially with girls who had been in school together since kindergarten. I felt uprooted, excluded, and anxious, just like I was feeling at the idea of moving away from the Bay Area.

Eventually, after years of trying to relocate in the outer world and years of being kidnapped in the dream world, I recognized that I was unwilling to leave the Bay Area. In an attempt to save my marriage, I found a beautiful home that seemed suited both to my husband and to myself. Fortunately, my husband liked the house and made the difficult concession to stay in the Bay Area. Once we bought our new home, I never dreamed about being kidnapped again.

An important addendum to this story is that in 2010, my husband retired. He had spent fifteen years in the Bay Area to be with me, and I knew that it was my turn to make a sacrifice. Although it was sad for me to leave a place where I had such deep roots, I didn't have one kidnapping dream. My unconscious knew that I wasn't abandoning something crucial by moving at this point in my life. I felt sad, but I didn't feel kidnapped.

The Runaway Bride

Another set of recurring dreams, bringing attention to a difficult life situation, came to Ann Mallin. From 2008–2012, Ann worked as a journalist at a major metropolitan newspaper. During these years, newspapers were reeling from the impact of the internet. Her newspaper, like others throughout the country, had lost its traditional relevance as the internet provided alternate sources of news and advertising. Ann was hired for the digital division of her newspaper as it struggled to keep up with the times.

Ann cared about the other journalists and respected their dedication to public service. She was excited to be on the cutting edge of technology in the news industry. However, by the time she had been at her paper for a year, she felt mounting anxiety during the day and had insomnia at night.

Although some of Ann's stress came from the 24/7 news cycle, the deepest source of stress for her was the anxiety in the newsroom. Waves of layoffs were occurring as the digital revolution and the recession wreaked havoc on the paper's finances. Every day, people came to work scared and those who survived the cuts watched as their colleagues' lives were torn apart. Ann often worked until the early hours of the morning and then returned to a demoralizing workplace the next day. During this time, Ann dreamed three times about a runaway bride. Two of those dreams follow.

> "Runaway Bride #1"
> *I'm a bride dressed in a beautiful, traditional gown and am at the church. It's my wedding day. But something inside of*

me doesn't want to be there or go through with it. I'm afraid I'll marry the wrong person. An independent contractor I had hired at work picks me up in a getaway car at the last minute and drives me to a secret location in the woods, where we hide out and eat french fries.

"Runaway Bride #2"
I'm dressed in a long beautiful gown and it is my wedding day. I am at the church, in the back dressing area. I feel panicked because I don't think I want to go through with it. My female family members who are in the dressing room with me, tell me, "You have to go through with it, we already bought the dress, and everyone is here." I look up at a TV screen in the corner (which shows and monitors what is going on inside the church). On the TV screen, I can see all the pews filled with people and the groom at the end of the altar, standing alone. I feel deep guilt for how I feel.

When Ann first had these recurring dreams, she thought they were about intimate relationships. She came from a traditional family where her mother and grandmothers had children by the time they were in their twenties and where there was no divorce. The presence of the traditional bridal gowns in both dreams didn't surprise her. Her life was unbalanced and part of her longed for a traditional family life. What she didn't understand was why her dream self was running away from something her waking self so deeply desired.

Eventually Ann shared her runaway-bride dreams with colleagues in her newsroom. When one asked if her dreams might actually be about work, Ann had an epiphany. As someone who was deeply invested in her work life, her work was like a marriage, but this was a troubled marriage and part of her, like the runaway bride, wanted to escape.

In her first dream, she and a colleague escaped from the wedding and hid out in the woods, eating french fries. The colleague in the dream was a friend who was particularly sensitive to stresses in the newsroom and who had encouraged Ann to develop other parts of her life. It made sense that she would help the runaway bride escape. Ann related to french fries as teenage comfort food. Perhaps part of her yearned for simple teenage comforts, far removed from the complicated and painful adult realities that surrounded her.

In the second dream, Ann felt guilty about her desire to run away. The television monitor was reminiscent of monitors in her newsroom as journalists continually watched cable television to keep up with breaking stories. The people waiting in the pews suggested the people she cared about in the newsroom, the people she would disappoint if she ran away.

Like many of our dreams, Ann's runaway bride dreams had more than one level of meaning. On a more literal level, the bride in her traditional dress expressed her longing for marriage and a more balanced life. She feared disappointing both herself and others if she didn't form a traditional marriage. However, the runaway bride was also a powerful symbol for the painful feelings she had about her work life.

Recurring Dreams of Completion

Another kind of recurring dream is one in which we try to resolve or complete a situation that ended painfully in our outer life. When we're not able to accept a failure or a painful ending in a life situation, we may return to it again and again in a dream. Although most of these situations can't be reversed in the outer world, we can reach resolution internally by grieving our lost opportunity and by finally accepting the course our life has taken.

Dreams of completion are reported by Jeni Gilbert, a corporate coach from Portland, Maine. When Jeni was nineteen she met her first husband, Pat. They had instant chemistry. Jeni still remembers how bashful they both felt at the heat between them. The two of them dated for two years and then Jeni began to lose interest in the relationship. Sensing that she was moving away from him, Pat proposed and Jeni unfortunately accepted. They were married for just short of two years.

Looking back, Jeni feels that Pat never gave her the feeling of connection that she needed. Nevertheless, she cared for him and felt sad that their relationship didn't work out. Over the years, she had many dreams where her dream self tried and repeatedly failed to make a deeper connection with Pat. She has sometimes felt confused about these dreams since she is in a satisfying second marriage where she receives what Pat couldn't give her. Here is a fragment of a dream where Jeni's dream self once again tried to connect with Pat:

> *I've remarried Pat. We're in a house that has a Spanish feel. We're in the kitchen. I ask him to put me on the countertop to kiss him. I like being up close to his face. We kiss, but he doesn't seem into it. I comment about being up on the counter, looking for agreement that it feels good. He responds by commenting on the colors of the walls and ceiling.*
>
> *I begin to believe I've made a mistake. The scene changes and I'm walking up a path to get food for dinner. It feels like I'm going to the facility where my current husband and I train coaches, although it's Spanish.*

Interestingly, the location of Jeni's dream shifted to the facility where she and her current husband now teach together. She was looking for dinner food there, perhaps able to get the nurturance in her current relationship that she couldn't find with Pat.

The facility had a Spanish feel to it. Jeni related this to the fact that she and her current husband now split their time between Maine and Spain. Jeni's dream held images of both past and present—a long-ago relationship still seeking resolution and the current relationship that she treasures.

Jeni reports that she shared this dream with her dream group in Maine and that the members suggested that she might not have fully grieved the loss of her first marriage. Jeni reports that, at their suggestion, she spent some time, fully experiencing that early loss. Since she has completed that inner work, Pat has not returned to her dream world. Her recurring dream is no longer needed.

In this chapter, we have looked at a variety of recurring dreams. Although the content of our recurring dreams may sometimes feel challenging, the intent behind them is comforting. It's deeply affirming to understand that our unconscious has our back. It continues to deliver the images that we need to heal and achieve greater wholeness.

Explorations

- Have you had dreams that have repeated during a particular life phase or even throughout your lifetime?
- What is the theme of those dreams and how do they relate to life preoccupations or to the issues in a particular life phase?
- What are the variations in those recurring dreams, and how do those variations reflect changes in how you are dealing with the underlying issue?
- What are your feelings about having these recurring dreams?
- When you focus attention on the issues underlying these dreams, do the dreams stop? If they don't, you haven't fully understood what your unconscious is trying to bring to consciousness.
- In your dream journal, indicate that this dream is recurring.
- If you feel frustrated about the repetition of a dream, consider reframing your response. Your unconscious is trying to help you resolve an issue.

Chapter Eight

Nightmare and Solace

It's a truism: Most of us like to feel energized and joyful, and prefer circumstances that encourage those feelings. Conversely, we dislike feeling stressed, anxious, and depressed. Yet, in spite of our strong preference for feeling good, many of our most important experiences occur in times of adversity. During our hard times, we sometimes discover internal resources or develop new skills that surprise us and help us to feel stronger and more confident. Loved ones and even strangers may step up and offer to help us in unanticipated ways. This unexpected assistance can result in us feeling more loved and more supported in the world. Although many of us have experienced gifts that come to us in dark times, there's no doubt that we prefer feeling good.

This preference in waking life extends to our dream life. "Sweet dreams" is something we routinely say to our loved ones before we go to bed. When we have a dream that comforts us, we wake up feeling happy and supported. When we have a dream that's stressful or frightening, we often say that we've had a bad dream and try to put it behind us as quickly as possible. If we have too many so-called bad dreams in a row, we can feel irritated or even angry. Although it's very human to create a duality between good and bad experiences, our difficult dreams can be as valuable to us as our difficult waking experiences. They can bring attention to something unresolved in our psyche and can help us to move forward with that issue.

One of my favorite Rumi poems encourages us to value the "bad" as well as the "good" in life and, by extension, in our dreams:

> This human being is a guest
> house. Every morning
> a new arrival.
>
> A joy, a depression, a meanness,
> some momentary awareness comes
> as an unexpected visitor.
> Welcome and attend them all!
> Even if they're a crowd of sorrows,
> who violently sweep your house
> empty of its furniture, still,
> treat each guest honorably.
> He may be clearing you out
> for some new delight.
>
> The dark thought, the shame, the malice,
> meet them at the door laughing,
> and invite them in.
>
> Be grateful for whatever comes,
> because each has been sent
> as a guide from beyond.

Welcome difficulty,
Learn the alchemy True Human
Beings know:
the moment you accept what troubles
you've been given, the door opens.[41]

Nightmares and the Integration of What We Fear

When we have a nightmare, our dream self, our waking self, or both experience anxiety, grief, and even terror. The subject of the nightmare can be trauma, as we saw in Susan's intruder dreams in Chapter Seven. The subject can also be any difficult situation in our inner or outer lives.

One of Carl Jung's most useful concepts is the *shadow.* As we navigate the social world, we develop a mask or *persona* that allows us to succeed in life. Our persona is shaped by social norms and ideals. Of course, many parts of our personality fall short of those ideals and we hide our shortcomings both from our selves and others. Our shadow is comprised of those parts of our character that we've rejected. Our nightmares are painful for us not only because they bring unresolved experiences to our attention; they're also painful because they bring our shadow into view.

Although our nightmares challenge us, they also offer an opportunity to resolve something that needs resolution. If we ignore the opportunity, we may have other dreams on the same uncomfortable theme or our dream may turn into a recurring dream. Our unconscious will continue to nudge us to integrate those things we would rather ignore.

Stalked

The imagery in our nightmares can be both palpable and disturbing. Sometimes the images in a nightmare may seem like an extension of daily life. At other times, the content of our nightmare can be monsters, threatening or threatened animals, or natural disasters. Although children may have more archetypal "boogeymen" and demons in their dreams, adults also have them.

A nightmare I had a few months before finishing this book illustrates how our nightmares can help us to move forward in life, even though we may not relish the experience of the dream. At the time of my dream, I was feeling exhausted and discouraged. I had spent a year interviewing dreamers, carrying out self-publishing tasks, and working with clients to support the book. I was tired, and when I ran into a series of problems with the book, I felt overwhelmed and doubted that I had the resources, internally or externally, to finish the project.

In the midst of this crisis of faith, I had a dream that I called "Stalked."

> *I'm in a place that at first seems like our current home. I'm in my bathrobe when the doorbell rings. When I answer it, I'm looking out through the locked security screen into the front yard where a man in a three-piece suit is piling boxes. He says that they're for me and that he'd like to bring them in. The security screen door is locked between us and I feel safe with that but I'm frightened. Even though he is well-groomed and well-dressed, I know that he's not what he appears to be. I know he wants to harm me. He's not just a criminal. He feels demonic in some way.*
>
> *I refuse him entry and go upstairs which is a different house. I'm trying to call 911 for back-up because I know this isn't over. However, there is no 911 anymore. I call a number randomly and ask for the number for emergency help. I'm given*

a number but when I call that number, it isn't in service either. There's no help and I'm alone in the house.

Meanwhile I'm on the second story of the house. I'm standing in front of a glass door. There's no lock on the door and on the other side, is the man in the three-piece suit. Only now he isn't alone. He has been joined by other men in three-piece suits with the same MO—demonic and well-groomed. I know that my future includes rape, pillage, and being murdered and there's nothing I can do. I'm out of defenses and have no resources to help me. I stand looking at these intruders who understand my vulnerability perfectly. We are staring at each other and then I wake myself up. I know I'm dreaming and I say to myself, "I must wake up. I don't want to go further with this nightmare."

Although I was able to stop the dream, I wasn't able to easily banish the demonic men from my consciousness. They lingered on, their presence very vivid to me. I felt frightened both in the dream and when I awakened.

As is my habit with a nightmare, I tried to engage with this dream as energetically, if not as happily, as I would engage with a more comforting dream. It wasn't difficult to see the parallel: I was stalked in my dream and I felt stalked by problems in my outer life.

The boxes in the dream were intriguing. They seemed like a gift, but were actually ruses the demons were using to get to me. This made metaphorical sense to me. I was feeling boxed in by a project that initially seemed like a gift, but felt like a burden at the moment. Since the demons were male, I wondered if my masculine stances of focus and drive were out of balance. My self-discipline looked well dressed and appropriate, but was it? Was I boxing myself in and did I need to rebalance?

Looking at the demonic figures as projections of my shadow, I asked myself, "How are my own attitudes demonic? How are my attitudes endangering me?" It seemed clear that old, childhood patterns of feeling unsupported and victimized were emerging. While I had not been able to nurture myself adequately as a child, I could as an adult.

After spending time with the dream, I began to respond to it with action in my outer life. I clearly laid out each area of the book where I was feeling overwhelmed and worked out steps to address each problem. As I dealt with each issue over the next few weeks, I felt less like I needed to call 911.

Most importantly, I headed up into the mountains to rest and to take stock of things. During the days of my retreat, I took long walks, ate healthy food, napped, and generally provided myself with the space to adjust my skewed attitudes. When I returned home, I had re-centered. I certainly remembered those demons, and probably always will, but their power over me had receded. I had responded to my scary dream and was ready for the final months of birthing this book.

David and the One-Two Punch

My intruder dreams provided impactful information about an important, but relatively minor, life passage. We also have nightmares that are big dreams. We may prefer big dreams in which we feel surrounded by loving presences, but we sometimes we need a stark and even horrifying reflection of the path we're on. While this kind of dream is no less a gift from the unconscious, it can be shocking. This is the case of two identical dreams reported by David Harris, a personal organizer, from Ventura, California.

At the time of these dreams, David was twenty-seven years old and already had a long history of drug and alcohol abuse. Filled with pain from a confusing and intolerable childhood, he had sought to escape his emotional pain by numbing out with substances. Starting out with cigarettes at age eleven, he soon added marijuana. By the time he was in his mid-teens, he was taking in anything he could "smoke, drop, and drink." His drugs of choice were barbiturates because they dulled his pain most effectively.

Although it seemed like he was on a downward spiral with no way up, a strong pull toward healing began to show itself. In his late teens and early twenties, David traded in Seconal (a barbiturate) for alcohol and later scaled down from hard alcohol to beer. At the time he had his dreams, he was drinking a couple of six packs of beer and smoking a few joints a week. As he describes it, he was trying to make himself into a functional alcoholic.

Here is David's twice-repeated dream as he was struggling to find the right relationship to his drug and alcohol abuse:

> *I am attempting to perform the simple act of walking across a barren, drab, featureless room, alone. To my helpless horror, I can't will my limbs to execute my commands. I'm moving in slow motion, as if through water, and looking at my arms and legs as though they're foreign, estranged entities. I know that they remember the familiar sensation of walking, and almost that they regret that they can't fulfill their usual function—but they're powerless over whatever force is denying them the ability to respond in their accustomed way.*
>
> *I'm lumbering, in slow motion, shocked, mystified and terrified. My form is half again as large as in real life, but misshapen, blunt, devolved, unrecognizable.*

David remembers these dreams as "a one-two punch." They had no softening plotline or cast of characters. Each dream presented him with the same extremely clear and visceral experience of his future body if he continued with his addictive behaviors. His misshapen and debilitated body was a time and a half larger than its normal size, emphasizing the painful destruction that awaited him.

The dreams of his physical deterioration, arriving when he was trying to refine his addictions, showed him the devastating outcomes of his current approach to drugs and alcohol. The visceral experience of his future deterioration shook him deeply. He realized that he was being shown an essential truth and that this was a fork in the road. He chose the road that led him to Alcoholics Anonymous and other 12 Step twelveprograms, where he worked the steps and used the tools offered by those programs. Eventually he experienced permanent freedom from alcohol, drugs, and other addictions.

David considers himself an obsessive person who first acted out that quality with his addictions. Since his life-saving dream, he has become obsessive about his healing. He has read hundreds of self-help books and goes to different forms of therapy or meditation five days a week. David tears up, even now, thirty-one years later, when he speaks of this dream. He believes that his deeper self allowed him to numb out in his younger years so that he could survive. When he was old enough and strong enough to begin to move away from drugs and alcohol, he was given a horrifying dream that saved his life.

A Life Filled with Dreams of Solace

Even when we understand the value of our nightmares, most of us prefer our dreams of solace. Fortunately, from childhood onward, our unconscious offers us dream imagery that inspires and comforts us.

Glenna Berry Horton, whose childhood dreams are presented in Chapter Four, estimates that she had dozens of childhood dreams about traveling to her grandmother's farm. Glenna not only looked forward to the next summer at the farm, she also dreamed regularly about traveling there. Her recurring dreams provided nurturing images that gave her strength to get through harsh Iowa winters and her weeks in the family sick room.

Glenna's unconscious continued to offer her many comforting dreams throughout her long life. When she was in her eighties, she had another meaningful dream of solace. At the time of this dream, Glenna had been involved with a man for several months. Wanting to become closer to him, she invited him to her ranch for a weekend. In preparation for his visit, she bought wine and delicious foods as well as concert tickets. However, just as he was scheduled to arrive, he called to break up with her.

Glenna felt the sting of this loss. She felt rejected and insecure about her attractiveness as an older woman. She was particularly vulnerable because of the deaths of her beloved husband and others close to her. In the midst of dealing with this painful break-up, she had the following dream.

> *My old thesis advisor and I are talking at the university but in the trappings of a tropical cabana. He says to me, "When you were my student, I used to step outside to see the sun playing in your hair."*

This dream brought immediate relief to Glenna. Her thesis advisor, a powerful man in her history, was remembering her hair and affirming her beauty. The choice of her hair was important since, as Glenna noted, her hair is still thick and luxuriant, unchanged by time.

Interestingly, the topic of Glenna's thesis was fatal attractions in Portuguese literature. In her waking life, her thesis advisor signed off on this project, validating that she was a survivor of the challenging thesis process, and that she had succeeded.

In looking at her dream, Glenna felt that she was being symbolically showed that she would survive this romantic defeat. She would survive her own fatal attraction. Since Glenna's painful relationship resulted in a new collection of erotic poetry about the affair, she, like the writers described in her thesis, used her painful experience to further her creative work.

A final detail of the dream was the setting—a tropical cabana. For Glenna, the tropics are "the seat of eroticism." The dream helped to heal the blow she had received by offering her advisor's validation and an erotic setting that was replenishing to her.

A Heavenly Dream

Our dreams of solace, like our nightmares, can present archetypal imagery as well as more earthy imagery to comfort us. John Connell, a media broker from Ventura, California, had the following important dream during a time of frustration and despair.

When John had this dream, he was in the midst of a financial crisis and general emotional despair. Like the journalist Ann Mallin in the last chapter, John had worked in an industry severely impacted by the internet. In 2006, he was employed by an agency that brokered deals between cable channels and manufacturers. He was doing well financially and felt good about supporting his growing family. Then the internet, with its marketing and purchasing capabilities, changed the landscape of television sales. Many cable channels lost their customer and advertising base, and folded. The few stations that remained created their own in-house brokering of deals. John's agency went under and he lost his job.

This began a lengthy period of financial distress for John and his family. His wife, new to her career as a psychotherapist, gave birth to their second child in 2007. The family then had two small children and no viable financial support. Although John started his own consulting business to do the brokering work he was good at, the work was patchy and didn't provide the steady paycheck the family needed.

John's dream occurred several years after the collapse of the cable marketing industry when he was still struggling to find his niche in the workplace. He was despairing about his ability to take care of his family. Complicating John's search to find work was his desire for work that would incorporate his spiritual values and would contribute to the well-being of the world.

He called this, "A Heavenly Dream."

> *I'm in a cathedral like I've witnessed at the Vatican. There's a huge ceremony underway with rows of beings dressed in robes like choral robes. Different groups are dressed in different colors. Hundreds of participants are on stage in lines. I find myself alone, dressed in what I remember as a white robe with a red frock. I'm holding a large book, scroll, or sign. I feel lost as I don't not know what line of participants to join.*
>
> *In the center of it all is an old man in white robes who shoots me a scornful glance because I'm not properly in place. It reminds me of how my father would look down the pew to silently reprimand me for fussing with the pencils or generally misbehaving, and I would shoot up straight to obey him.*
>
> *I'm at a loss about what I am supposed to do or where I am to go so I take refuge in approaching a participant at the end of the rows. As I approach him, he seems to grow in size until he is like a giant. He looks down at me with a whimsical smile. He is gloriously handsome, bearded, with long hair that surrounds his smiling face. He seems to assure me to not worry but to just proceed. I completely trust his kindly reassurance. His big beautiful hands come to rest on my shoulders and he gently and lovingly turns me to face a different direction. Before I can make a decision about where to align myself in the assembly, my dream shifts and the scene disappears.*

John's dream, set in an otherworldly cathedral, expressed his deeply spiritual nature. His dilemma in the dream, like that in the outer world, was finding his right place. There were many different groupings of people, but he didn't know where he belonged. He didn't know where to get in line.

John's first encounter in the dream was with a priest dressed in white. This dream character expressed disapproval of John and embodied the painful judgment John was feeling toward himself. John then encountered a beautiful, angelic being whom he called The Advocate. The Advocate grew larger right before John's eyes, becoming an angelic giant. His compassionate and smiling face brought a sense of calm to John. His huge, loving hands gently turned John in a different direction, providing the re-orientation he needed in his inner and outer lives.

An interesting aspect of the dream was that The Advocate didn't point John toward a specific line to join. That was left open. The reorientation had more to do with relaxing into greater self-acceptance and greater trust in God and his journey. John was encouraged not to worry, just to proceed.

After this dream, John still struggled to find the right way to bring in the steady paycheck he needed, but his attitude changed due to his encounter with the angelic being in his dream. He felt calmer about figuring things out. The dream didn't solve his problem, but it shifted the despair that contributed to the problem.

As of this writing, John reports that he has been hired as a media broker with a company that allows him to work remotely. This job gives him the opportunity to earn good money while caring for his children after school when his wife is working. The job also leaves him some time to pursue the spiritual interests that are important to him.

Welcoming All of Our Dreams

In this chapter, we've seen how nightmares and dreams of solace offer equal help in the unfolding of our life. Although it is certainly more enjoyable to engage with heavenly figures than with demonic stalkers, both kinds of imagery offer guidance. Our task is to remember this truth when we feel disturbed by the content of a nightmare and want nothing more than to forget that dream as quickly as possible. When we "treat each guest honorably," we live in the guest house envisioned by Rumi and can participate more fully in the unfolding of our own destiny.

Explorations

- Remember a nightmare that you've had. What was your response to it when you awoke? Did you try to distance from it or wish that you hadn't had it?
- Remember a recent nightmare that you tried to avoid. Go to a comfortable place in your home and write the dream down. Be gentle with yourself. If you feel anxious, calm yourself with your favored techniques for self-soothing.
- What are the themes and feelings in that dream? How do they relate to themes and feelings in your waking life at the time of the dream?
- Do the characters in the dream remind you of people in your life or of shadow parts of yourself?
- What kind of actions in your waking life might help the waking dilemmas brought to your attention in the dream?
- Remember that it's important to acknowledge your shadow parts, to treat them honorably, while at the same time diminishing their harmful impact on your life.
- Do the same explorations with a dream of solace. Notice that you may feel more enthusiastic about exploring this dream.

Chapter Nine

Healing in the Dream World

As we have seen throughout this book, many of our dreams lead us beyond our limited waking perspectives, helping us to achieve greater balance and wholeness. In addition to receiving dreams that promote emotional health and balance, we also have dreams specifically related to physical illness and healing the body. Sometimes these dreams are diagnostic and precognitive, informing us of a physical condition before it has been diagnosed. At other times, our dreams offer information about what we need to heal a physical illness or provide solace when a condition can't be changed. We also can receive in-dream healing that helps to resolve physical illnesses. Our ability to receive information about physical health and to experience actual healing in the dream world has been reported throughout history.

Asklepian Dream Incubation

Perhaps the most powerful tradition of dream healing in recorded history occurred in the temples of Asklepios in ancient Greece. From 1200 BCE to 600 CE, supplicants with intractable mental and physical illnesses traveled to sanctuaries for in-dream encounters with Asklepios, the gentle god of healing. Although Asklepios' primary temple was at Epidaurus (600 BCE–300 CE), there were large healing centers at Kos and Pergamum as well as at hundreds of smaller Asklepian sites for supplicants unable to travel to the larger sanctuaries.

The healing offered in the Asklepian temples is what we today would call holistic. Cleansing baths in spring water, exercise, herbs, and therapeutic conversation with temple priests purified the supplicant and prepared him for an in-dream encounter with Asklepios. When the supplicant was deemed ready for the divine encounter, he entered into the *abaton*, an underground chamber with beds for dreaming. Here, tucked away from the world, the supplicant awaited the divine meeting that would relieve his suffering. Conversations afterward with the temple priest helped to clarify the path forward, based on the guidance received in the dream.[12]

It's important to note that for the ancient Greeks, tending or incubating dreams prepared the supplicant for a very real experience in another dimension. The desired in-dream meeting was viewed as an actual encounter with a god, not as a dialogue with the unconscious. If the god appeared in one of his various forms—boy, dog, or serpent—these forms were viewed as different manifestations of the god, not as metaphors or vivid images needing to be explored.

Many believe that the tradition of Asklepian healing began with the work of a wise and beloved physician who practiced medicine in Thessaly around 1300 BCE. After the physician's death, his followers carried his medical practices from the mountains of Thessaly south and he was honored as the greatest healer in the Mediterranean world.

As time went on, a myth of divine origins grew around the human doctor. In this mythic tale, Asklepios was the offspring of an affair between of Apollo, God of Healing and Prophecy, and Coronis, a princess of Thessaly. Later, when Coronis had an affair with a mortal man, the jealous Apollo had her killed. However, in a fit of remorse, he rescued his infant son from the belly of his mother as she burned on her funeral pyre.

According to myth, Apollo, after rescuing his son, gave him to the centaur Chiron, a master of the healing arts. Chiron taught Asklepios the use of herbs, incantations, and healing waters. Asklepios offered these healing gifts to the human race, adding to them the cultivation of healing dreams. Over time, Asklepios became one of the most beloved of the Greek gods. A Homeric hymn sings his praises:

> Of the healer of diseases, Asclepius, I begin to sing, the son of Apollo, whom fair Coronis bore in the Dorian plain, the daughter of King Phlegyas, a great joy to men was her son, and soother of evil pains. Even so do thou hail, O Prince, I pray to thee in my song.[43]

Contemporary Dream Healing

The healings at the Asklepian temples were grounded in Greek culture, mythology, and medical practices. Very few modern people seek a dream encounter with an ancient Greek god and there are unfortunately no incubation centers available to us today. However, the core experiences of Asklepian healing are still very much alive in the human psyche. We still receive diagnostic and prescriptive information from a realm beyond our waking state. The process of dream healing may be cloaked in different stories and images, but we still have dream encounters with healing forces that astonish and humble us.

In my own life, I have had one diagnostic dream related to breast cancer. When I was sixty-two, I was preparing for my yearly mammogram. My mother died of breast cancer and I had been having a yearly mammogram since I was forty. I had been fortunate to have many years of clear scans and was fairly blasé about the yearly test. In 2012, I awoke from a dream and heard the words, "Something is wrong in your left breast." Trusting my dreams as I do, I was certain that my upcoming mammogram would show cancer, and it did.

Fortunately, my tumor was small and caught early. I received good medical care, and after a lumpectomy and MammoSite radiation, I was able to close this relatively short chapter of my medical life. The dream itself, however, has had far-reaching consequences. My dream diagnosis of a tiny, undetectable tumor gave me confidence that my unconscious is monitoring my body and that my dreams will deliver messages about the state of my body.

The following diagnostic dream came to Carole Petiet, a nurse and psychologist who lives in the San Francisco Bay Area. Not only did Carole have an unshakeable belief in the accuracy of her dream's diagnosis, she also had the courage to insist on receiving medical treatment based on that dream.

A Fierce Belief in Her Dreams

When Carole was thirty-one years old, she had an upper respiratory infection that lasted for weeks. During this time, she went several times to urgent care at the healthcare center where she was employed as a staff psychologist. Because she was otherwise fit and athletic, the doctors weren't worried about her condition. Eventually she was prescribed antibiotics, and yet even with this assistance, her condition worsened until she could only sleep sitting up and was unable to go to work.

In August, Carole pulled herself together and went to Los Angeles to deliver a paper at a psychological conference. After she presented her paper, she fell into bed, depleted and ill, and had the following dream:

> *I am in an oxygen tent. It is very steamy in there and I am hooked up to IV antibiotics so that I won't die.*

Awakening with a start, Carole recognized the treatment protocol she was receiving in the dream was for pneumonia. She returned immediately to the Bay Area and went to her healthcare center, letting the doctor on duty know that she felt certain that she had pneumonia. Taking in Carole's healthy appearance and listening to lungs that sounded clear, the doctor disagreed with her and diagnosed a nasty virus.

Given her dream from the night before, Carole felt certain that she had pneumonia that would get progressively worse without prompt treatment. She asked for an X-ray. As a member of the medical profession herself, she understood that the doctor would ridicule her if he knew a dream was the source of her certainty, and as a result, she didn't share her dream with him. She and her doctor had words. He was sure she didn't have pneumonia. She was sure that she did. When Carole persisted and made it clear that she wasn't leaving until the X-ray was taken, the doctor finally relented.

Some time later, he returned. "My tail is between my legs. You do have pneumonia. Although you sounded clear, your whole right lung is impacted. I have never seen anything like this and so have done some research. You have what is called an atypical viral pneumonia. The medicine you are on is for a bacterial infection and you need medicine that treats a viral infection instead. Get this medication, and if you aren't better soon, come back."

After two days on the new medication, Carole was on her way back to health. Of the dream that diagnosed her, Carole says, "I was so grateful to my unconscious for diagnosing physically what was happening inside my body, in a language that I, as a nurse, understood."

Mimi's Miscarriage

While Carole's dream presented a clear diagnosis that could be addressed with proper medical care, Mimi Nelson Oliver had a dream predicting an unavoidable miscarriage. At the time of the dream, Mimi, a clinical social worker from Massachusetts, was in her early forties. Her dream provided spiritual solace that helped her through an irreversible and heartbreaking situation.

During her twenties and thirties, Mimi went through a long struggle with infertility. She received intensive fertility treatments as she and her husband tried to have a child. During those difficult years, she had two miscarriages which were devastating. When her body couldn't carry through with what she considered her birthright and her destiny, she was plunged into spiritual despair about the meaning of her life.

Eventually Mimi found ways to work with her losses. She and her husband adopted a son whom she adores. She also began to study various forms of holistic healing and developed a program called FertilEnergy. Connected to a fertility clinic in Danvers, Massachusetts, Mimi's program supported women and couples who were experiencing the stresses of fertility treatments.

When Mimi was in her early forties, she was stronger physically, emotionally, and spiritually due to the work she had done to heal her earlier losses. Feeling as good as she did, she began to work with her fertility doctor again and became pregnant. Six to eight weeks into her pregnancy, she had the following dream that foretold her third, and final, miscarriage.

> *I am walking alone, though I feel loving presences around me on all sides. 'We' are walking in a beautiful hillside valley, in a luscious field of colorful wildflowers. I'm wearing a long, flowing white lace sundress. My hair is blowing in the wind. I momentarily feel blissful, alive, full . . . a glorious feeling that I have never felt before.*

Then out of nowhere, a very minute red speck appears on my very white dress. It startles me. I continue to walk, a little more slowly, a little less blissful, still hopeful but then knowing as the spot grows into a blotch, until the red consumes a large part of the bottom of the dress. I collapse in shock, then despair.

When Mimi woke up from her dream, she understood that she was going to miscarry, and of course felt the loss and despair she had felt with her previous miscarriages. However, she didn't plunge into the same spiritual crisis. Because of the presences she felt all about her in her dream, she felt watched over and cared for as she experienced this loss.

In addition to preparing her for her miscarriage and giving her support, Mimi's dream was an important step in her spiritual development. At different times throughout her life, she had felt surrounded by loving, spiritual forces. However, as she says, "I had felt them, but it is so easy for me to forget." Her dream strengthened her belief that spiritual support is always there, even when she forgets it.

Mimi's final miscarriage, foretold by her dream, ended her long struggle to carry a child. However, her engagement with this issue continued in her own healing and in the professional work she offers to others. The day of her miscarriage, in spite of her own loss, she met with clients at an important FertilEnergy group. Since that program ended, she has spent many years as a clinical social worker at Mass General, including nine years as an obstetrical social worker. Today she carries her hard-won understanding of pregnancy and infertility issues into her work with clients.

A Journey Through Cancer

Dale Figtree, a nutritionist and author from Santa Barbara, California, reports a series of powerful, lifesaving dreams that began when she was in her twenties. Some of these dreams were precognitive. She called the first dream “An Offer of Help”:

> *I am in my childhood house with Sai Baba, a great Hindu holy man. He offers to cure me of a problem in the left part of my chest by operating on me. I have the sense he wants to reach in and pull something out—like a small marble. I agree to this and lie down, but then quickly bolt upright and ask, “Where are your tools?” He laughs and says his hands are his tools. I lie down for another moment, then spring up again and ask, “Where is the antiseptic?” He laughs again, calming me and tells me not to worry. I lie back down once more, but then quickly rise again and ask, “Where is the anesthesia?” As he attempts to soothe my doubts, I cross my arms in front of my chest and say, “Don’t touch me.”*

When Dale had this dream, she was mystified. She knew vaguely of Sai Baba, an Indian holy man. She had no idea why she was dreaming about him. She only knew that in her dream she didn’t trust him and didn’t want his help.

Two years later, while Dale was living in New York City in a spiritual community led by a teacher named Joya, an X-ray revealed an abnormality in Dale’s chest cavity. After testing, she underwent thoracic surgery and a malignant lymphatic tumor was found attached to her heart, left lung, and main arteries, literally choking off her life force. The tumor was deemed too dangerous to remove and the surgeon sewed Dale back up again, leaving the tumor untouched except for a biopsy.

Shortly after this surgery, Dale remembered the dream she had had of Sai Baba two years earlier and remembered that he wanted to “operate” in the same area where her tumor had recently been found. Memory of this dream threw Dale into despair. She wondered if she could have avoided her life-threatening illness and the devastating treatments for her cancer if she had accepted Sai Baba's help.

After surgery, Dale followed through with the various treatments Western medicine offers. She underwent two months of chemotherapy and six months of five-day-a-week radiation. At the end of these treatments, her tumor had decreased from the size of a grapefruit to the size of a walnut. However, the surrounding tissue was so badly damaged from radiation that even her small tumor was inoperable. Dale's doctor regretfully told her that Western medicine had done all that it could do for her, leaving her with a dire prognosis.

This was a defining moment for Dale. Filled with fear that she was on her own, she realized that if she wanted to live, she would have to find her own way. In retrospect, this was the moment when she stepped up, taking responsibility for her own physical, mental, and spiritual healing. She now believes that she didn't accept help from Sai Baba because her spiritual task was to take responsibility for her own life and to empower her own healing on every level.

Once Dale began to search for different healing modalities, resources poured in from many directions. Yoga, meditation, and visualization became part of her path to healing. Perhaps the most significant help came from Dr. Gian Cursio, a Naturopath who taught that the human body is built to heal itself and, if given proper nutrients, will do just that. Dale began Dr. Cursio's prescribed diet of 70% raw food and three vegetable drinks a day, a diet which today, forty years later, she still follows closely.

A few months after Dale began her nutritional program, she went back to see her oncologist, who was greatly puzzled. Although he had believed she had a very negative prognosis, her tumor had not grown and her bloodwork was good.

During this phase of her healing, Dale had the following dream, which she called "Food at Sea."

I am in the middle of a great ocean, drifting in a small rowboat. A big ocean liner comes by and rescues me. I then find myself in the dining room of the boat, starved from not having eaten in days. With my eyes, I am carefully inspecting some cakes with thick icing that are inside a glass case. My mouth salivates as I look from one cake to another. Suddenly I straighten up and speak to the waiter, saying, "I would like a big salad, please."

Dale was cognizant that the image of drifting at sea can occur close to death. In her dream, she was drifting toward the end of her life, but fortunately was rescued by an ocean liner. Once on board, she turned away from sugar-laden food temptations toward a salad. For Dale, this dream validated her nutritional program as a powerful force in her healing.

Six months after this dream of being saved at sea, Dale had thc following experience of in-dream healing that she called "Damn Pea."

I am with my spiritual teacher Joya and say to her, "There is only a pea-size piece of cancer left in my body, only a damn pea!" She says "Open your shirt and let me pluck it out." I say, "No, I'll do it." Joya says, "Don't be stupid. Open your shirt." Again I say "No," but then I finally realize that if I could do it myself, then why was the cancer still there! I go ahead and open my shirt. Joya reaches in and pulls out the pea and says, "There, done!"

Unlike in the earlier dream with Sai Baba, Dale now accepted the offered help. She was still reluctant, but realized that she could not heal the cancer on her own. In spite of fully engaging with mainstream and alternative approaches, she still had cancer in her body. If she was going to survive, she needed to humble herself and take the help that she once refused, this time offered by a woman she trusted.

During the three years following these dreams of nutritional and spiritual assistance, Dale went through many ups and downs, including a four-month healing crisis during which she ran a constant fever and lost thirty pounds, weighing in at only ninety pounds. After finally recovering, her body had changed significantly. Her weight was redistributed, and her hair, skin, and nails were healthier. Most dramatically, a CT scan showed her to be cancer-free. Her tumor had disappeared and has never returned.

After undergoing this remarkable healing, Dale began to receive calls from people from all over the country who had heard about her healing and wanted her help. She eventually went back to school and obtained a doctorate in nutrition. For the past forty years, she has used the tools and approaches that saved her own life to help many others.

Dale's healing dreams are at base a mystery. As has been noted many times in this book, dreams and the unconscious remain ultimately unknowable. Was Dale visited first by Sai Baba and later by Joya in the dream world? Did these teachers offer the help that she finally accepted? Seth, who described the dream world as a separate dimension of reality where we can be visited by other beings, might have accepted this interpretation. Jung, on the other hand, might have viewed Sai Baba and Joya as archetypes, embodying healing energies from the collective unconscious. Dale herself leans toward the belief that powerful spiritual teachers visited her in the dream world.

Regardless of interpretation, Dale's healing involved both a 100% commitment to her own empowerment and healing, and a surrender to healing forces beyond those of her waking self. Through the dynamic interplay of will and surrender, body and spirit, a remarkable healing occurred. Dale's journey has, of course, marked her. Scarring from the radiation treatments remains challenging. However, her healing and the dreams that were part of it have allowed her forty years of freedom to live life deeply and to help others.

In this chapter we've seen a variety of ways that dreams aid our healing: through diagnosis, through offering soothing or frightening imagery that motivates us to change how we treat our body, and perhaps through in-dream healing that directly addresses our illness.

The various ways that dreams can assist our healing process were accepted in many indigenous cultures as well as in the practices of ancient Greece. In these cultures, healing wasn't left totally to dreams. Trained healers had special skills to help alleviate suffering through herbs, surgeries, and other healthful practices. However, it was also believed that important information about diagnosis and treatment was available to the patient in the dream world. The dreaming self, with its access to that other realm, was viewed as an important partner in our healing.

Today we tend to project the archetype of healing onto a human physician and to discount our intuition and our dreams, important resources for our healing. The dream stories in this chapter reveal the powerful contributions our dreams are capable of making to our health.

Explorations

- Think back over your dream history. Have you had a dream that predicted a physical illness, or a dream that has commented on treatment you were receiving for a diagnosed condition?
- Going forward, notice any dreams that specify a part of the body. If you dream of an animal attacking or gnawing at a particular part of your body, if you dream of being wounded in a particular part of your body, pay attention. This dream image may be metaphorical. However, the unconscious maybe sending a message about a physical condition.
- If you have had a dream about an attack on a part of the body, notice if you are feeling discomfort in that part of your body or have any other indications that something is wrong. If you feel uneasy, consider talking to your health care provider. While medical professionals may balk at information presented in dreams, they are often open to hearing that a patient has an intuitive sense that something is wrong.
- When you are receiving treatment for a condition, notice if your dreams provide any commentary on your treatment. For instance, if you begin a new medication, and have a dream of a helpful woman, that may indicate that your body is responding to the medication. A dream with a negative or frightening image might indicate the opposite.

Chapter Ten

The Final Gateway

Even when we are in the midst of life, death is waiting in the wings and, at any moment, can step onto center stage and take over our life. Facing the death of someone we love is excruciating and letting go of life itself is the biggest task we face. Fortunately, we receive unexpected gifts as we approach the challenges of the final gateway. One of those gifts is our dream life. Our dreams can help us heal our relationship to those we love while they are dying and after they are gone. Our dreams can also help us shift our relationship to death and ease our crossing over when it's time to leave this life.

Navigating the Death of a Loved One

Valerie McCarney, a hospice volunteer and expressive-arts facilitator from Saratoga, New York, had a remarkable series of dreams that demonstrate how dreams can help us connect more deeply with those we love as they are dying. Her dreams show how dreams can help to heal strained relationships and bring comfort to the dying.

Valerie's first dream in this sequence was about a family gathering. This dream came to her on the morning of her fifty-sixth birthday. At the time of the dream, Valerie was dealing with overwhelming life circumstances. In addition to her mother's terminal illness, her father was dying and her husband was battling cancer. She also had a full work life, serving hospice patients and kids at group homes and schools. Valerie felt depleted and overwhelmed, and had no time to process the demanding events in her life or to replenish herself.

In the midst of this stressful time, Valerie had a dream which she called "A Birthday Dream." In the first part of this dream, she was at a party in her childhood home on Long Island. In the latter part of the dream, she was at Mastic Beach, New York, a place her mother loved. During the course of the dream, Valerie encountered many people, both living and dead, who were important to her. She interacted with relatives on both her mother's and father's sides of the family, with her daughter, and with her lifelong friend, Dot. In the fragment of her dream that follows, Valerie connected with women on her mother's side of the family.

> *My birthday and what a dream I had. I'm in my childhood home on Long Island. There's a big family party in our finished basement. I walk down the stairs and look around at the crowd. Everyone is there—the living and the dead. Sitting on her old chair is Nana, my maternal great grandmother, who died when I was two. I know her from a bit of memory, but mostly from the old pictures.*
>
> *My maternal grandmother is also there laughing and talking to her mother. I say, "Oh my God what a surprise, Nana is here." I go up to Nana and hug her. She's a very small, thin woman with a thick Irish accent. She looks at me but I can tell she doesn't know who I am. I just keep hugging her and saying, "Oh Nana, I'm so happy to see you."*
>
> *I also see my Great Aunt Margie standing next to Nana. She looks like she did in the 1950s and 60s. Her hair is dyed*

bright red and she has on a satin green striped dress. She was an unmarried, working woman who lived in Manhattan and who always looked like a model. She just looks at me, no smile. I think, "Oh no, she has not forgiven me for not coming to the hospital just before she died."

I turn back to look at Nana and see that she's now under a big old oak claw-foot table. I say, "Oh my God, why did she go under the table?" Nana's eyes are open but she isn't speaking. People come up and are looking at her as if looking at a newborn baby behind glass in a nursery. Nana is looking around. Her eyes look so much like my mother's when she was listless with an infection and fever several years ago.

My mother is standing next to me in perfect health, cooking. We're both watching Nana and glance at each other, concerned about her. I say to her, "Wow, I never knew that Nana looked so much like you." She says, "No, you look like her. "

I'm so excited to see everyone. I just keep looking at everyone's faces and understand what a gift this is because some of them are dead, though no one seems to know or care.

Valerie's dream was immediately comforting to her. Being connected to her relatives in places important to her family reminded her of feeling safe and loved as a child. She remembered the laughter and the good times. These reminders were soothing, helping her to feel supported by both the living and the dead during this difficult period in her life.

The powerful solace provided by this dream moved to a different level when Valerie received a birthday call from her mother shortly after she awoke. Valerie's mother had had a stroke eight years before and was now living in a nursing home. She was extremely debilitated and slept much of the day. She sometimes was alert and communicated clearly, but often was in a different reality. Valerie hadn't received a birthday call from her mother in three years and wasn't expecting one on her fifty-sixth birthday. She was more than surprised when her mother called to wish her a happy birthday.

The bigger surprise came after Valerie told her mother that she had had a dream of being in Mastic Beach with all the relatives. Hearing this, her mother became very quiet and then told Valerie she had had the same dream. The two of them excitedly shared the encounters they each had had with the same relatives. Valerie's mother told Valerie, "I always go to Mastic in my dreams," something Valerie hadn't known.

In the time leading up to their mutual dream, Valerie's mother had been morose—fearing her own death and grieving the impending death of a brother she loved. Being able to talk about happy childhood memories lifted her mood. Valerie had been struggling to find a way to help her mother. As she watched her mother's mood improve as they talked about their dreams, Valerie saw that it was important to strengthen her mother's connection to these earlier times at the beach.

This shared dream opened a new intimacy between the two of them. As a child, Valerie had been strong-willed and rebellious as her mother experimented, sometimes unsuccessfully, with parenting Valerie, her first child. Valerie's years as a "wild child" during the 1960s hadn't helped their relationship. Much later, when her mother became ill and depressed, Valerie had wanted to comfort her. However, the tension between them had prevented Valerie from connecting with her in a more meaningful way.

After experiencing this shared dream, a new chapter opened between them. When Valerie visited each week, she asked her mother about her memories of the beach. Valerie brought her mother a small sandbox with a miniature rake and shells, as well as old family photographs. Aided by these prompts, her mother was able to connect more deeply with her love of the beach and with her happier childhood memories. When her mother wasn't able to interact much with words, she ran the sand through her fingers and was comforted.

One day, Valerie's mother commented, "I wonder why we didn't get along for so long?" Valerie answered, "I don't know, but the important thing is that we do now."

Six months after the party dream, Valerie's mother entered the hospital where she spent the last two weeks of her life. Valerie was with her for most of those two weeks. On her mother's last night, Valerie's cousin, an ICU nurse on duty, said, "Your mother is stable. Why don't you go home for your husband's birthday?" Valerie followed that suggestion and went home. That night, Valerie had a dream that told her that her mother was crossing over.

I'm in my childhood home and go down to the basement. It's empty and dark except for a closet light. I'm down there for only a minute when the feeling comes over me that I'm being watched. I look around at the doors to the boiler room, the laundry room, and the old pantry, and think, "Oh no, there are a lot of places to hide and someone is watching me."

My heart starts to beat fast and I'm scared but I don't want to show that to whomever is watching me. I then look down at the floor and see a glittery butterfly. I wonder if it's painted on the floor or maybe it's a brooch? I say to whomever is there, "Oh, I will just go upstairs and get some cleaner to clean off the floor." Of course, I have no intention of coming back down.

I run to the top of the stairs and before I close the door, I look back down. I see a huge vision of my mother with all the tubes sticking out of her. I gasp, and say, "The angel of death is in the house." I startle awake, sitting upright.

After this dream, Valerie sketched what she had seen. Feeling better, she went back to bed, but as soon as she put her head on the pillow the phone rang. It was her cousin telling her that her mother was actively dying. Valerie jumped into her car, but didn't make it back to the hospital before her mother died.

Later Valerie went over to her mother's house to pick up some clothes for the funeral. When she opened the top drawer of her mother's bureau, she found a glittery butterfly brooch—just like the butterfly that had appeared in the dream. Valerie doesn't remember ever having seen that brooch before.

Valerie grieved the death of her mother, but she was helped by the dreams and the synchronicity of the butterfly brooch. In their times "at the beach," she and her mother had said everything that needed to be said between them. Valerie also felt that her mother had come to say her final goodbye to her in her dream. Their relationship had healed and was complete.

Valerie's party dream and her butterfly brooch dream were bookends. The party dream initiated a cycle of healing for Valerie and her mother. Previously, they had been locked in difficult patterns that their waking selves were unable to shift. Sharing a mutual dream created a connection that arose from a deeper part of themselves, and allowed Valerie to comfort her mother as she was dying.

The butterfly dream let Valerie know that the work was done and her mother was crossing over. The butterfly, a universal symbol of transformation, was an apt symbol for her mother's final transformation and for the transformation that occurred in the relationship between Valerie and her mother. Now years later, Valerie still wonders at the dreams and the synchronicities that occurred during the time leading to her mother's death.

As a footnote, Valerie's dreams and her time with her mother have had ripple effects. She has talked about this experience with many people in workshops she has facilitated and her account of this experience has been included in various books. Valerie's dream story has inspired many people about the power of dreams and the possibility of healing difficult relationships in the months leading up to death.

Prartho Receives Help in Letting Go

Valerie's dreams helped her connect with her dying mother in a way that surprised and comforted her. Our dreams can also help us grieve and let go after a loved one has died. This was the case in dreams that Prartho Sereno had after her father died.

When Prartho, a San Francisco Bay Area poet, was twenty-eight, she lost her father. For almost a year, she dreamed of him often as she grieved the loss of him in her life. Toward the end of that time of bereavement, she had the following dream:

> *In my dream, my father comes toward me and I remember that he is dead. I actually become excited because I think he might be able to tell me where he is and the process of getting there. I'm afraid to ask though, feeling it might be against some cosmic rule. However, I lean toward him and ask, "What is on the Other Side?"*
>
> *He looks at me with deep love and empathy. I can still see the pure blue of his eyes. He leans in toward me and opens his mouth. Out comes, "Awaa nban pahh muut ma bley . . ." I strain to hear better and he strains to enunciate more clearly, but we both come to the realization at the same time that we now speak different languages and will not understand one another. At the end of the dream, my father's face is sad, but no less loving.*

This dream was a turning point for Prartho. She understood that she and her father were now existing in different realms, and that that was how it should be. The dream was also a confirmation of the unknowable—there are things about life and death that we are not meant to understand as long as we are in a human body. In experiencing these things so clearly in her dream, something inside of Prartho relaxed. She was able move on, feeling loved by her father, but also more separate from him.

Making Peace with Death

Perhaps the most challenging task we human beings face is living with the fact our own death. It's a challenge to meet the demands of our unique unfolding, while understanding that we will eventually lose everything we've worked hard to create. If we focus too much on the inevitable end of life, we can feel terror and paralysis, and fail to fulfill our destiny.

Many of us live with these tensions by adopting religious or spiritual beliefs that help us to live with the fact of the final gateway we must pass through. A belief in an afterlife or in reincarnation helps many people to achieve greater spiritual security. Creating a relationship to death that allows us to live successfully is an important developmental task.

Sometimes our dreams can help us develop a relationship with death that allows us to realize our unique destiny. When we examined the life of the medium Jane Roberts, we saw the experiments she undertook in the dream world. Learning to fly free of the body in sleep helped to corroborate the views of her teacher Seth—that we are multidimensional beings existing in a multidimensional universe. Roberts's own experiences in the dream world helped shift her own views of reality, but also gave her the "proof" she needed to fulfill her destiny as the person who delivered the Seth Material.

Three Dreams About Death

When Wilma Friesema, a social worker and writer from Oahu, Hawaii was in her thirties, she had a series of three dreams that had a profound impact on her views of life and death.

The child of Dutch immigrants, Wilma was raised in the Christian Reformed Church in Michigan. The Christian views of this denomination stressed a strict code of behavior in order to avoid hell and enter heaven after death.

As an adolescent, Wilma left the church, and in her twenties and thirties she began to search for her own form of spirituality. Her explorations led to a few years of study with an East Indian guru. This exploration was followed by training in Transpersonal Psychology, an approach that adds the spiritual dimension of experience to more traditional views.

During this period of intensive searching, Wilma had a sequence of dreams about death. These dreams presented an experience of death very different from that portrayed in her early church experience. These dreams lessened her anxiety about death and created a greater freedom to live her life authentically.

In this sequence of dreams, Wilma's experience of death progressed from terror about dying in the first dream to a peak experience in the third dream.

> "Death Dream #1"
> *There are soldiers with machine guns chasing me down. I run into a house, up some stairs, and hide in a closet. I'm terrified. They find me and shoot me dead. It's painful and very frightening. I'm aware that I'm dreaming and remember being told, in waking life, that if you die in a dream you actually will die so I think I'm truly dying. I feel lost and very afraid. My spirit starts to leave my body and it's excruciating. I'm terrified. I wake up, shaken and surprised to still be alive.*

"Death Dream #2"
I'm with some friends and we're walking down a side street in a city. We get accosted by robbers who want our money. I refuse to give them my purse and one of the robbers stabs me, several times. I'm bleeding profusely and I know I'm going to die. This time, I don't feel as frightened, and the letting go of my physical body is much easier. I'm surprised, but it doesn't feel traumatic, just natural. I feel a general sense of well-being and peace.

"Death Dream #3"
I see a friend walking along a path in a forest. I'm looking from above, but it feels like I'm right next to him. He's talking intently and I'm listening, but then I realize I'm dead. I had just died recently, but it had been so painless I hadn't noticed. With that realization I'm flooded with a profound experience of joy and expansiveness, like I had tapped into the universe's current of life and its ecstasy was flowing through me. It felt similar, but bigger, to the peak experiences I had in my waking life. It was such a deep and profound sense of well-being and love.

Wilma considers these to have been big dreams because of their profound effect on her life. She notes that in the first dream, she was aware of the spiritual platitude that we can't dream about dying without actually dying. Because of this platitude, she was terrified that she had actually died and wouldn't wake up. When she did wake up, she felt affirmed in her growing trust in her own experience and her own sense of what is true, rather than following an external belief system.

This teaching in the first dream laid the groundwork for the final two dreams of being released into a state of peace and love. All of the platitudes about death she had learned as a child were far from her own experience in these dreams. There was no judgment of good and bad, no admission to heaven or sentencing to hell. Rather, there was a natural opening to another level of being, a state of peace and ecstasy, free of a human body.

This unexpected experience of death in the last two dreams shifted Wilma's views of death. Old fears of judgment or of annihilation, planted in her from early childhood, began to melt away. At the same time, she felt released from the view that we must live in certain constricted ways in order to avoid damnation.

Wilma states that like everyone else, she doesn't know what happens after death. She also doesn't know if these dreams will bring comfort to her as she approaches her actual death. However, these dreams have helped her to detach from fear-based messages about death and to live in a more authentic way.

Dreaming Toward the Final Gateway

As we approach our death, we struggle to find peace as our body declines and as we are called to let go of everything we have valued, including life itself. Our religious and spiritual beliefs may be challenged as we face this task. During this last arc of life, our dreams continue to offer us support and guidance.

Dolores Cummings, Valerie McCarney's mother, had many dreams during the last six months of her life. As we have seen, she dreamed often of Mastic Beach, New York, where she had many wonderful childhood experiences. In these dreams, she interacted with relatives, living and dead. These dreams comforted her, particularly after Valerie helped to anchor the dreams in this world with old pictures and beach memorabilia.

During her last weeks in a hospital room, Dolores talked about dreams of flying out of her room to visit people. She also had many dreams about her brother, Buddy, who died shortly before her. She sometimes confused her dreams about Buddy with actual phone conversations with him in her waking life. Although she didn't spend time with him physically, her dreams kept him close to her in her last months.

A final dream, which Dolores had in her last days, is a classic dream of a relative coming to fetch us as we approach death. The "I" in this dream is Valerie, Dolores' daughter.

> My mother saw her father, my grandfather. He was wearing his Italian tee shirt and old pants, and was standing by the swinging door in the ICU, staring at her. She pretended she didn't know he was dead in the dream, but did wonder why he was dressed in the way he dressed on hot summer nights at home.
>
> I asked her if he said anything. She said, "No," but that he motioned her to come and opened one of the swinging doors. Mom, however, didn't want to go through the doors. When she said and did nothing, he just stood at the door looking at her.

Although Dolores didn't follow her father through the swinging doors during this dream, she did go through the final gateway soon after.

Final Dreams

Our last dreams, that come to us in the days before we die, help us to let go of life. Because people close to death are in an altered state of consciousness, they don't write down their dreams. However, their dreams are reported by nurses and clergy, hospice workers, and family members. People who have sat with the dying have noted how dreams help us to complete this life and cross over with greater serenity. The recurring themes in these final dreams include, being on a journey, a life review, the presence of companions and guides on the journey, and an encounter with a comforting, luminous light.

A Beautiful Hotel

When my own mother was dying, she had a joyous dream of traveling. This dream occurred two or three days before her death, when she was turned inward and transitioning.

At the time of this dream, I had been with her for almost three weeks. I had witnessed her last telephone calls to lifelong friends, her last visit with her hospice nurse, her last glass of evening wine with my father, and her final retreat to her bed. Her metastatic breast cancer had left her barely more than a skeleton, but she was mostly at peace during these final weeks. Given that I had not always been an easy daughter for her, I was glad to be able to join with my father, caregivers, and other family members to help her during this final phase of her life.

As I sat by her bedside during the days before she died, I watched how her eyes sometimes moved back and forth like a person in REM sleep. From her sounds, I could tell that she was having experiences in the dream world. A couple of days before she died, I became incorporated into her dream world as she began to speak aloud the words she was saying in her dream. Her voice was very young, like that of an excited four- or five-year old. "This hotel is so beautiful," she exclaimed. "Look at the marble floor and those wood bannisters, and look at the light coming through the windows. Look at all the people here."

I believe she then made her way to her room in the hotel because she said, "This room is so nice. Look at that pretty bedspread. Are these pretty soaps for me, just for me?" I took her question, asked aloud, to be an invitation to participate in her dream and answered, "Yes, yes, these soaps for you, just for you."

In her journey away from this life, my mother found a symbol of a journey that made her transition both safe and wondrous. Although she had often felt disappointed and dissatisfied during her life, she now was an excited and joyful child whose needs were being met.

It was healing for me to contribute to this dream and to help the sweet, vulnerable child receive what she needed—something that was for her alone, not needing to be shared. Some of my own disappointment in our relationship disappeared as I was able to connect with her in a new way. The pain and tension between us lessened—a gift of the dream world to the living and the dying.

Path of Light

John Sanford, author of *Dreams: God's Forgotten Language,* wrote of a powerful dream that his father had a couple of days before he died. This dream contained two of the elements that frequently occur in our final dreams: a life review and the presence of a brilliant, comforting light.

Sanford's father, like John Sanford himself, was an Episcopal priest. After working as an engineer and Latin teacher in the States and China, the senior Sanford found his vocation as a priest and tended parishes in New Jersey and Massachusetts for thirty years.

During the last years of his life, Sanford's father suffered from a heart condition and eventually struggled with kidney failure. In and out of the hospital, he was in a good deal of pain. During this time, he became depressed and anxious about death. Sanford wrote of his father's challenging experience, "Priest or not, every one of us is just a human being and during one of these bitter illnesses he told me of his own anxiety about death . . ."[44]

A week before his death, Sanford's father had an important dream that he shared with his wife. After experiencing this dream, his anxiety left him and he faced his death with serenity. The "he" in the dream is Sanford's father's dream self and the "I" is his mother who recorded the dream.

> *In the dream, he awakened in his living room. But then the room changed and he was back in his room in the old house in Vermont as a child. Again the room changed: to Connecticut (where he had his first job) to China, to Pennsylvania (where he often visited) to New Jersey, and then back to the living room. In each scene after China, I was present, in each instance being of a different age in accordance with the time represented. Finally he sees himself lying on the couch back in the living room. I am descending the stairs and the doctor is in the room. The doctor says, "Oh, he's gone." Then, as others fade in the dream, he sees the clock on the mantelpiece: the hands have been moving, but now they stop; as they stop a window opens behind the mantelpiece clock and a bright light shines through. The opening widens into a door and the light becomes a brilliant path. He walks out on the path of light and disappears.*[45]

The clock's presence in this crossing-over dream was a meaningful symbol. In the first part of the dream, the dreamer made a journey backward in earthly time, exploring the different periods in his life and remembering his wife at different times in their life together. After this life review, he returned to present time and heard the announcement of his death. As the physical world faded, he saw a path of light, opening up behind the clock. This path led into an unknown dimension of time and space in the future. The clock was an apt symbol for the time travel in this dream: from past to present to the future. As with Wilma Friesema's dreams about death, there was the suggestion that death is not the end, but rather is an opening to another level of profound experience.

The light present in this dream is encountered in the dreams of many as they approach death. This luminous presence is also described by mystics and by those who have had near-death experiences. "It Felt Love," a short poem by the fourteenth-century Persian poet Hafiz, describes the divine light that helps us to take the next step in our development and that helped Sanford's father achieve peace in the days before his death.

How
Did the rose
Ever open its heart

And give to the world
All its
Beauty?

It felt the encouragement of light
Against its
Being.

Otherwise,
We all remain

Too

Frightened.[46]

After Sanford's father's death, his family commemorated his life and his final dream by engraving the words "path of light" on his headstone. This dream image not only prepared the dreamer for death, it also brought solace to a grieving family.

The Power of Our Dreams About Death

As we approach death, our dreams continue to guide us. They can help us release painful, and seemingly intractable, patterns in our relationship to loved ones who are dying. They can help us with our grief after someone has died. Our dreams also help us to reshape our relationship to death, both as we live out our lives and as we are actively engaged in dying. Our dreams accompany us until the end of our days.

Explorations

- Have you had dreams about your own death? How have they affected your relationship to death and to your life?

- Have you been close to anyone in the last stages of life or in their final days? Have they shared any dreams with you?

- If loved ones have shared dreams in their last months of life, have these dreams showed how you could bring them greater comfort?

- If loved ones have shared dreams in their final days, have they had the themes we have seen in this chapter: a final journey, a life review, the presence of guides to help them cross over, the the presence of a luminous light?

- As those you love approach death, be open to their dreams. While you can be aware of the themes of this chapter, the most important thing is to be open and present to their dreams.

- The same goes for dreams as you approach your own death. Be open to them. We need all the help we can get at the end of life and our dreams don't fail us.

Chapter Eleven

Visitations

Every dream takes place in another dimension of reality, in a place that isn't of this world. In that sense, every dream is an expansive experience that leads us beyond the limitations of our waking self and the physical world. Although every dream takes place in another dimension of reality, our dreams are most often populated by people, places, and images that are related to this world. Sometimes these people and places are known to us and sometimes not, but they are clearly connected to Earth.

Another kind of dream connects us with beings not of this world. We encounter the dead who are no longer here, or meet beings and creatures that have never existed on Earth. Otherworldly dream encounters feel like visitations from other levels of reality and add another level of meaning to our dream lives. Although there can be dramatic action in some visitation dreams, there often is a close-up, one-on-one interaction with another being. Sometimes we're offered specific counsel during these visitations, and sometimes the presence of the otherworldly being is itself the message. When we have an otherworldly visitation, we feel like we've engaged with something bigger than our waking selves. We can feel soothed, inspired, or blessed.

In *Extraordinary Dreams and How to Work with Them*, Stanley Krippner, Fariba Bogzaran, and André Percia De Carvalho wrote of visitation dreams:

> In visitation dreams, a deceased person or an entity from a spiritual realm (or even an "alien" from a UFO) reportedly provides counsel or direction that the dreamer finds of comfort or value. Sometimes the dreamer visits a domain that transcends his or her ordinary reality, learning about matters that involve the most profound aspects of the human psyche. Visitation dreams seem to represent a transpersonal reality only dimly perceived by human beings. They create a way in which the dreamer can either be visited by an inhabitant of this realm, or called to make a journey to this realm, encountering a deceased loved one, an angel, a spirit, or deity. These dreams are mythic in nature; like myths, they focus on existential concerns and have consequences for the dreamer's behavior. The message from the otherworldly visitor can change the dreamer's life.[47]

Dawn's Birth Mother Pays A Final Visit

A common kind of visitation dream is an encounter with a loved one while he is crossing over or after his death. In the last chapter, we saw Valerie McCarney's dream encounter with her dying mother and Prartho Sereno's dream of attempting to communicate with her dead father. Dawn Nelson Barankin also had a visitation dream at the time of her birth mother's death. This visitation dream offered a haunting image and was an important step in resolving the wound between her mother and herself.

Dawn is an author, educator, and workshop leader from Walnut Creek, California. In 1991, she founded Compassionate Touch for those in Later Life Stages™, a program offering massage and gentle touch to the elderly, the ill, and the dying.

Dawn's own infancy in Kentucky was traumatic. Juvenile Services was called repeatedly by neighbors in her apartment building, who reported a child left alone and crying. When Dawn was thirteen months old, her mother abandoned her for three days. Police broke into the apartment and found Dawn dehydrated, hungry, and untended, and she was taken immediately to the hospital.

Dawn's mother was arrested and the courts awarded custody to her paternal grandparents, as her father was serving in World War II overseas. This began a childhood of living in many different situations—with her grandparents, with her father and his changing wives, and in a children's home in Kansas for eighteen months. Some periods were better than others, but change was a constant throughout her childhood.

When Dawn was seventeen, she met her birth mother for the first time. Although she was a teenager who already had too many adults in her life, she was curious to see if she was anything like her mother. Their connection was obvious when they appeared, dressed very similarly and reading the same book. Her mother, who had a lifelong struggle with alcoholism, was sober at the time, and the two of them took the first steps toward forming a relationship.

However, after this beginning, Dawn's contact with her mother was intermittent over the next two decades. Dawn remembers visiting her in a trailer park in Florida where she was living with a boyfriend. It became clear that her mother had started drinking again. In the middle of the night, Dawn was awakened by the sounds of a verbal fight that was turning physical. When a gun was mentioned, Dawn fled to a neighbor's home to sleep before heading home as quickly as possible the next day.

When Dawn was thirty-four, she had her final meeting with her mother, who was dying of cancer in a hospital in Florida. Three weeks later, Dawn experienced a vivid and powerful visitation dream. She believes that this visitation occurred during or close to the time that her mother was transitioning out of her body.

> *My birth mother appears, standing at the foot of my bed. She is wearing a long white garment, something between a wedding dress and a nightgown. A double row of heavy chains hangs from shackles around each of her wrists, dropping down to the ground. She looks distraught and a bit angry and confused. I sit up in my bed, looking at her directly, and then say, spontaneously, "I forgive you." I repeat this a number of times. Eventually her demeanor softens and the chains fall to the ground as her image gradually fades.*

After this dream encounter, Dawn felt that something had completed itself in her relationship to her mother. Although the image of her mother in chains was a bit shocking, it was also exhilarating in a certain way. She felt gratitude that her mother had reached out at the time of her transition. She felt thankful for the opportunity to say "I forgive you," and hoped that she had helped to ease her mother's passing.

Although this dream marked a significant step in resolving Dawn's early trauma, the dream wasn't the end of her work on her relationship with her mother. Over the years, she has engaged in a variety of therapeutic and meditative practices that have supported her healing. She is currently working on a memoir. As part of her research, she has acquired court documents revealing new details in regard to her early situation. This new information has helped her to access her sadness and anger on a deeper level and to move forward in her inner work.

An important part of Dawn's healing has also occurred in her own family life, where she has created the stable attachments and love that she lacked in childhood. She is in a forty-year marriage and is close to her three adult children and her grandchildren.

In reflecting on her life, Dawn is moved by how her wounding helped shape her personality, and how her trauma led to a life of psychological and spiritual growth. Her work, bringing touch to those lacking adequate physical and emotional connectedness, was almost certainly influenced by her own early deprivation. Given the connection between her early trauma and the rich development of her life, Dawn resonates with this line from Rumi: "The wound is the place where the Light enters you."

Jacob's Ladder

In addition to interacting with our dead in our visitation dreams, we often interact with otherworldly beings who have never inhabited this world. In many religious traditions, there are accounts of dreamers being visited by angels, gods, or celestial beings. Those of a Jungian persuasion might see these celestial beings as archetypes, universal figures that arise from our collective unconscious to help us on our journey. Others, with religious or metaphysical viewpoints, might view these dreams as actual encounters with non-physical beings who are reaching out to us. In the Sethian worldview, the dream world is an actual location where beings from other realms, as well as the dead, can pay us a visit. While some of our dream encounters are metaphorical, others are actual visits. A famous visitation dream in the Judeo-Christian tradition is the biblical dream of Jacob's Ladder.

Jacob was the son of Isaac and Rebekah. Toward the end of his life, the blind and ailing Isaac prepared to pass his blessing and the legacy of leadership on to his eldest son, Esau. Rebekah and Jacob, the younger son, were unwilling to accept this traditional transfer of power. They schemed to disguise Jacob as Esau so that he would receive the blessing. Isaac was deceived and Jacob received the blessing meant for his brother.

When Esau found out about this deception, he was enraged and plotted to kill his brother. Getting wind of this, Rebekah convinced Isaac to send Jacob out of Canaan, to marry into her own people to the east. Isaac blessed this new endeavor, and Jacob left his home land, his community, and his family. Shortly after his departure, he had the following dream:

> And he lighted upon a certain place, and tarried there all night, because the sun was set; and he took the stones of that place, and put them for his pillow, and lay down in that place to sleep.
>
> And he dreamed, and behold a ladder set up on the earth, and the top of it reached to heaven: and behold the angels of God ascending and descending on it.
>
> And, behold, the Lord stood above it, and said, I am the Lord God of Abraham thy father, and the God of Isaac: the land wherein thou liest to thee I will give it, and to thy seed:
>
> And thy seed shall be as the dust of the earth, and thou shalt spread abroad to the west, and to the east, and to the north and to the south: and in thee and in thy seed shall all the families of the earth be blessed.
>
> And behold, I am with thee, and will keep thee in all places whither thou goest and will bring thee again into this land; for I will not leave thee, until I have done that which I have spoken to thee of.[48]

We are told that upon awakening from this dream, Jacob took the stone he had used as a pillow and set it up as a pillar.

He then anointed it with oil, as a symbol of God's house and of the covenant between himself and God.

Jacob's dream was clearly a big dream that provided a vision that guided the rest of his life. We can imagine that he may have felt somewhat guilty about having robbed his brother of his inheritance. He may also have felt unmoored and afraid as he left his home lands, his community, and his family to travel into the unknown. This dream provided spiritual solace in a time of transition.

The imagery of this visitation was compelling and universal. The ladder is a symbol of bridging—in this case between heaven and earth, the holy and the mundane. The visitation of angels ascending and descending was also powerful. The angels weren't just descending, they were also ascending, suggesting a dialogue between the earthly and the spiritual. Finally, God appeared, offering protection and a vision of the future of Jacob and his progeny. With its bridging between the earthly and the divine, this dream offered a personal covenant between Jacob and God. This dream was as big a dream as we humans have. It's no wonder that the dream still holds power, over two thousand years later.

Archangel Michael Takes the Wheel

Dreams of angels are not exclusive to the Bible or to scriptural figures. Throughout human history, people have dreamed of visitations by angels. In Chapter Eight, we saw John Connell's dream of The Advocate, an angelic being who took John by the shoulders and gently turned him in another direction. When John awoke, he felt reoriented in his life and was able to face his life challenges with greater equanimity.

Lisanna Rood, a clinical social worker from Santa Barbara, California, is a spiritual seeker who has explored different religions and spiritual traditions. The following dream of the Angel Michael was important to her both spiritually and emotionally:

I'm the driver of a car but am sitting in the back seat, and am unable to reach the steering wheel or pedals. Archangel Michael shows up. He is blond and angelically handsome, at least seven feet tall. He slips into the driver's seat and takes over the wheel for me. What is most striking about the dream is that I actually can feel his presence.

At the time of this dream, Lisanna was exploring the experience of being loved and supported by angels. Although she had been raised in a religious Jewish family, she had always felt uncertain about her relationship to God. Feeling loved by angels was a new experience for her. She was particularly drawn to the Archangel Michael. This dream added to her growing sense of spiritual security. She felt cared for by a large and strong being who showed up when she needed him and who was rock solid. She was on a path of relaxing into an experience of greater love and this dream was an important step on that journey.

This visitation also provided Lisanna with renewed emotional security. When she was seventeen, her father died unexpectedly from an aneurism. He was fifty-seven years old and left behind seven children, the youngest of whom was only eight years old. The loss of her father, a warm and expressive man, was a devastating blow to Lisanna, her family, and their community.

After his death, Lisanna felt more vulnerable in the world, with only her mother left to care for the family. She sensed her father's loving presence in the non-physical world, but still had a sense of vulnerability and insecurity. When she had this dream, part of her felt held and healed, as if a father figure reassured her that she was never alone.

Lisanna's visitation dream offered her spiritual and emotional support. The energy she felt in the dream was so vivid that she still clearly remembers it. She still draws support from the image of an angel who took charge when her own feet couldn't reach the pedals.

Meeting John the Witch

The otherworldly figures that come to us can also lie outside religious traditions. In the following dream I encountered two otherworldly characters, an otherworldly witch and a small black creature that was part cat and part dog. Although my dream character insisted on being called a witch, he was very like John Connell's Advocate and Lisanna Rood's archangel in both his appearance and the energy he emanated. I named this dream "Meeting John the Witch; A Spiritual Adventure."

> *I'm in the basement of a large building. It's like a boarded-up warehouse. The rooms are very large and filled with covered furniture and industrial machinery. I'm in this space with some other people, mostly men, and am accompanied by a small black creature that sometimes seems like a dog, sometimes a cat, and sometimes a hybrid of both. I pick her up sometimes when there seems to be a danger to her.*
>
> *I begin to feel the presence of another, non-physical presence in the room. At one point, I look into a mirror and see, out of the corner of my eyes, a being with long hair. At first, I think it's a woman, but then can dimly perceive a man.*
>
> *I find this unseen being's book of spells in the room. It's a beautiful book with poems and water colors. It doesn't have to do with spells in the ordinary sense.*
>
> *As I pay more attention to the being, he becomes increasingly vivid until I can both see and communicate with him clearly. He's an absolutely gorgeous, otherworldly being, at least seven feet tall with long white hair. He has the most beautiful, luminous blue eyes, like nothing I've ever seen in this*

world. I notice that every time I ask him the right question or intuit something correctly my body elevates so that I am looking at him eye to eye.

When I ask him if he's my teacher, he says he's not, but that we're connected. It appears that he is the teacher of one of the men in the room, a kind of clueless man who might be a soldier. I'm sad that he's not my teacher, but am happy to have met him. I'm so happy that such a beautiful being exists.

At the time I had this dream, things were going well in my personal life. I was enjoying my life in Ventura and was in a period of steady, enjoyable work on the book. However, I was disturbed by the political climate in the United States. The polarization between the right and left wings of the country, the ongoing scandals, and the erosion of respect for the rule of law and for diversity were deeply troubling to me. Throughout my life, I have thought that we are a disturbingly primitive species, and have hoped that there are more evolved beings out there in the universe. During this time, I particularly hoped that we humans are not the apex of creation.

Dreaming about John was a healing experience. His luminosity and beauty were stunning. He was everything I wish that we humans were. At the same time, he wasn't perfect. His book of spells didn't contain spells in the usual sense. The book contained poems and pictures, the output of a processing, evolving being.

It was interesting to me that John was called a witch. When I tried to call him something other than a witch, my unconscious insisted on labeling him that. When I think of witches, I think of those who are adept at bending or manipulating the forces of the universe for good or nefarious purposes. The fact that John was a witch said to me that he was skilled at understanding the laws of energy and creation. His book of spells was about understanding the deeper structure of the universe, and shifting energy creatively. I also noticed that this picture of a witch was very different from my encounter with an evil female witch at age three (see Chapter Four). Clearly my experience of power had evolved.

Another interesting thing was that I could rise to meet John at his level if I asked the right question or had the right intuition. This was a reminder that evolving is not about having all the answers. It's about asking the right questions and being open to intuitive forms of knowing.

The little hybrid dog/cat was a creature from somewhere else. In waking life, I was between pets, and was considering whether to adopt a dog or a cat. The dream gave me an animal that was a hybrid. However, the deeper meaning of this animal was that it alerted me that I was in an otherworldly place.

When I have a dream about otherworldly beings or places, my map of the geography and the inhabitants of the inner world becomes more detailed. My sense of the universe and its possibilities expands and I feel comforted about the possibilities for our further evolution as a species. This dream brought me that kind of comfort. John the Witch is now a part of me, just as people in my waking life are part of me.

Extraterrestrials in Her Living Room

Another common kind of visitation dream presents extraterrestrials. Jeni Gilbert, a coach and corporate trainer from Portland, Maine, experienced a significant visitation dream during a time of change. For the two years prior to this dream, Jeni had been feeling more open, less bound by fear. She had forged a close connection to a family in Spain, a country she loves. She had been traveling there twice a year, learning Spanish, and looking forward to a time when she could live there part-time.

Jeni's new sense of adventure was surprising and delightful to her, and the first thing she noted about her dream was how little fear she had when she encountered the extraterrestrials. When anxiety arose in relation to them, she was able to work with it. This attitude in her dream closely paralleled her growing ability to work with anxiety and take risks in her outer life.

Jeni's dream follows:

John [her husband] and I are at home, although not the same layout as our current house. A small plane is circling, and moving in different directions in the neighborhood. It looks like a light-blue Cessna. It begins to approach our house, flying lower, then comes in closer. I'm a bit concerned it's going to crash or land near us.

Then it flies in really low, heading for us, before transforming as it lands in the living room. Its landing is vertical like a helicopter. It's now a large black rectangle shape—a UFO.

I'm a bit anxious, although not really scared. I'm curious too. There's a large flat screen on it, and images appear. At first there are voices that I don't understand, and briefly seems there are images of beings that are strange, like out of a science fiction movie.

A voice speaks, in English, and somehow surmises my fear and wants to know why I'm afraid. I tell it that we've had TV shows and movies over the decades about ETs and they've all come to earth to harm us. They reassure me that they're not here to harm us, and I relax.

Below the screen are books on shelves and I ask if I can look at them. Some are closed with string, and have something handwritten across the binding in another language. The man tells me to lean my head against the screen, like mind melding, to assess if it's OK for me to read the books. It seems like I must be intelligent enough. I must pass because he gives me permission.

At times, the voice in the box seems like a man's voice and at other times, like a woman's. At some point, these beings are no longer in the box, but out in the room with me. I spend time talking to a woman, admire her clothing, and ask if I can touch it. It seems like the dream is in black and white. The clothing/fabric is beautiful. It's simple, but I'm attracted to the weave.

I ask her what they (the extraterrestrials) really look like, presuming they've changed shape to look like us. With some trepidation, she offers to show me and I say yes. She sends for a small being, I think it's a child. She's adorable. I don't recall seeing her face, but the center of her body is a pattern, like it's made out of simple lace. I'm really taken with her.

I fantasize about going to their planet with them. I ask, or want to ask, how long it took them to get here. I think about John and I being apart and wonder how that will be for us? Will we see each other again? Then the woman asks if I want to go for a short ride? It would be for fun. I wouldn't have to leave completely. I say, "Yes!"

Jeni approached this dream both as a metaphor and as an encounter with otherworldly, spiritual forces. As a metaphor, she noted the connection between her outer-life explorations and the dream. The extraterrestrials' books were in a different language and paralleled learning a new language and culture in her outer life. The mind-meld, to test if she was ready to read the books, seemed similar to tests in her outer world. Had she developed enough strength to follow through with her new life?

The detail of the lacy torso of the extraterrestrial child was intriguing. Jeni associated lace with frivolity. Lace adds beauty to life, but isn't essential to survival. For many years, Jeni had focused on meeting responsibilities as she raised children and ran her own business. Her love of Spain was a draw to something beautiful, but not connected to responsibility. She felt that the young extraterrestrial girl might represent a developing part of herself that was connected to beauty and adventure, independent of heavy responsibilities.

Another important detail was that John, Jeni's husband, faded in the dream. He wasn't included in the decision to visit the extraterrestrials' planet. However, she was concerned about her connection with him and wondered if they would see each other again.

In the outer world, John wasn't as interested in Spain as Jeni, and her explorations there were somewhat independent of him. She and John have worked together as corporate trainers and are very close in their marriage. In her life, she was concerned about how her developing life in Spain would impact their relationship. Her dream reflected this worry.

Although Jeni understood the metaphorical meanings in her dream, a metaphorical approach didn't fully explain why her current situation was framed as a visit from extraterrestrials. Jeni noted that in meditation, she has experienced the presence of a committee of beings from another realm. She has sensed them offering her counsel and guidance. Although Jeni doesn't have any particular religious beliefs, she feels that there are realities beyond the physical world. The extraterrestrials reminded her of spiritual realities and opportunities just out of sight.

In Jeni's dream, she was offered new experiences—connection with extraterrestrials, books in a different language, and a journey to another dimension of reality. As anxiety arose, she worked with it so that she could move forward in her explorations. This dream presented a spiritual snapshot of Jeni. She is becoming more adventurous and moving courageously forward on her path.

A Glimpse into Other Dimensions

Our visitation dreams are particularly suggestive. In addition to their possible metaphorical interpretation, they suggest a universe filled with spiritual mysteries and non-human beings. Some dreamers feel that their visitation dreams might be metaphorical or connected with the collective unconscious. This was Jeni Gilberts's sense of her dream about extraterrestrials. Other dreamers, such as Dawn Nelson Barankin, feel that their dream was an encounter with a separate being, no metaphor involved. No matter where we fall on this spectrum of interpretation, visitation dreams make us feel like we have been touched by a greater transpersonal force. We feel we have glimpsed into a universe alive with more expansive possibilities.

Explorations

- Have you had a dream where your interactions seemed more like a visitation than a metaphorical drama?
- Write down that dream and reflect on the qualities of that dream. What distinguished it as a visitation dream?
- Were there other creatures in that dream, or a setting that let you know that you were in a different dimension of reality?
- What was the teaching in that visitation dream?
- What has been the impact of that visitation dream on your life?
- When you reflect on that dream, does it shift your view of the nature of reality and of your place in the universe?

Chapter Twelve

Sharing Our Dreams

At first glance, dreaming seems like one of our most solitary pursuits. While we dream, our inner senses are activated. Our shared social world falls away and we focus on non-physical dimensions of experience. When we later awaken with perplexing dream imagery, we may not see the point in sharing seemingly senseless imagery with others. And even if we enjoy the inner work of engaging with our dream imagery, this focus may seem like another aspect of dreaming that sets us apart from other people.

And yet, in spite of the seemingly solitary nature of dreaming, we humans have always come together to deepen our connection to the dream world and to receive guidance. In indigenous cultures throughout the world, we have turned to shamans and other strong dreamers to bring guidance from the dream world. We have gone on vision quests in search of dreams to guide our lives, and have shared those important dreams with our communities. In Ancient Greece, we traveled to healing centers to incubate our dreams and to receive guidance from the god, Asklepios. Like other human beings in human history, we moderns have a strong desire to make our dreaming part of our collective experience and have developed ways of sharing our dreams.

The Kin of Ata Are Waiting

One of the most delightful books about sharing dreams is a novel, *The Kin Of Ata Are Waiting For You*, by Dorothy Bryant. In this story, a violent and morally corrupt man commits a murder. As he tries to escape from the scene of his crime, he's in a serious automobile accident. When he awakens, he finds himself in a very different world.

Ata, the place where he awakens, is a world devoted to dreaming. Every aspect of life is structured to support attunement to the dream world, which is viewed as the true reality. The people of Ata sleep in in a circle on the floor with their feet pointed together like spokes of a wheel. Upon awakening, their first act is to pair off to share their dreams. From toddlers to old people, everyone participates in this morning ritual. In this time of shared dreams, guidance for the individual as well as the community is communicated and becomes part of their social fabric. Once a dream is communicated, the dreamer and the community seek to implement the guidance in the dream in waking life.

Throughout their days, the kin of Ata remain focused on their dreams. Engaged in subsistence farming, they work just the right amount to remain focused on the dream world. Working the right amount is *nagdeo*, good for dreaming. Working too much and becoming exhausted and distracted is *donagdeo,* or bad for dreaming.

Similarly, moral conduct is based on how it affects dreaming. When the inevitable anger and irritation between people emerge, the kin of Ata withdraw into an underground chamber where the individual purges his upset emotions and returns to the calm state needed to stay attuned to the dream world.

This mythic tale follows the transformation of the main character as his violence and greed gradually lessen. Although he makes many mistakes, he slowly evolves into a strong dreamer, devoted to living in connection to the greater spiritual reality that dreams point toward.

It is, of course, unlikely that many of us will live in a utopian society like the one described in this book. However, this inspirational tale reflects our human desire to integrate our dreams into our life with others. The story also demonstrates specific ways of living closely connected to the dream world. Living in a moderate way to support inner attunement, sharing our dreams consistently with others, and implementing the guidance of dreams in the physical world, are useful takeaways from this story.

In the modern world, the people we live with offer the first opportunity for sharing our dream world. Lovers, roommates, and family members are the people we wake up with. Having an interest in one another's dreams is a primary way of honoring and strengthening our dream lives. Particularly powerful is the family unit, where encouraging children to share their dreams can create lifelong habits of valuing and sharing dreams.

Sharing Dreams in the Connell Family

The Connell family lives in Ventura, California. Laurel works as a psychotherapist and John as a media broker. Jack, their son, is fifteen and in ninth grade. Isabel, their daughter, is eleven and in sixth grade. Their family also includes a dog, a cat, a turtle, a lizard, a rabbit, and a hamster.

Both Laurel and John have been strong dreamers since childhood. Laurel grew up outside of Philadelphia in a household focused on personal self-expression and spiritual development. Her father was a chiropractor, her mother a massage therapist. Both of her parents were interested in past lives and holistic living. Although the family didn't share dreams, Laurel was encouraged to share all of her experiences, including dreams.

When she was ten, she had a vivid dream about trying to save children in World War II (see Chapter Four).

John was raised in an Irish Catholic family in Massachusetts. Although there were strict rules for keeping six rambunctious kids in check, his parents also encouraged personal expression. Each night at dinner, his father went around the table and gave each child an opportunity to tell about his day. In best Irish tradition, good storytelling was valued. Although John's parents weren't dreamworkers, John occasionally shared his dreams as part of the dinner check-in. The kids also occasionally mentioned dreams in the morning as they watched TV. John's first powerful flying dream occurred when he was five.

When John and Laurel came together as a couple, each of them was committed to spiritual development and open communication. Since they both followed their own dreams, sharing dreams was a natural part of being with each other. When they had children, they encouraged their kids to openly share their life experiences, including their dreams. When their children were little, the family cuddled in bed on weekend mornings, and Laurel and John shared their own dreams as part of that time together. As the children grew older, they began to share their own dreams. From an early age, Isabel was interested in her dreams and related them to her family. Jack shared his dreams as a small child, but grew more private about them as he grew older.

Today, sharing dreams is part of beginning the day together. Laurel often brings coffee to John in bed, and then John, Laurel, and Isabel chat as they prepare for their day. Dreams are one thread of that conversation. On the weekends, Isabel and her parents still have a family cuddle in bed and again, any dreams are welcomed into their morning chatter. John, Laurel, and Isabel report that they all become excited when one of them has a powerful dream, particularly a visitation dream from a dead family member.

Having received encouragement from an early age, Isabel has a rich dream life that she communicates with ease and enthusiasm. She remembers a dream of skiing with her paternal grandfather who died when she was one. This dream was as vivid as any experience in the physical world and helped her to bond with a grandparent she didn't know in her waking life.

Another favorite dream was of school friends on a boat in a jungle at Disneyland. The day after having this dream, Isabel discovered that these friends had been at Disneyland the day before and had been on the boat ride that was in her dream.

One of Isabel's most interesting dream experiences is a recurring dream. When she was six, she had her first dream of being a little girl living in Africa in a different family made up of a mother and sister. Since that initial dream, she has had many others. Each dream has offered a slightly different perspective on that African life. Compared with California, her world in Africa is simple, with fewer opportunities. She and her family are extremely poor and yet there is love and tenderness between them.

When Isabel was ten, she wrote a short story about a young African girl's experience of war and peace. This story was an elaboration of her dream experiences. The story won a prize in a national writing contest.

Another significant experience, connected to her African dreams, occurred with the family dog. Isabel often makes up names for the family pets. A year ago, she began calling their dog Gariki Garu. She believed this was a set of affectionate nonsense syllables. One day, Jack looked up the words "gariki garu" on Google Translate and found that they mean "blessed dog" in Swahili. This synchronicity was powerful for the whole family and validated that Isabel's Africa dreams tap into a past or parallel life.

As years of sharing dreams pass, the Connells find that their dreams are as distinct as their waking personalities. John often dreams of himself as a superhero, performing amazing feats.

These dreams inspire him to take risks in life and to strive to be his best self. He regularly has out-of-body and flying dreams.

Laurel's dreams tend to be closely related to the themes and emotions of her waking life. She also has many dreams where she dies. Although the circumstances surrounding her death vary, she has the repeated experience of death being less stressful than she expects. Her unconscious seems to be helping her make peace with her own death.

Isabel, like her mother, has dreams connected with the feelings and experiences of her waking life. Also like her mother, she has precognitive dreams where she experiences things that haven't yet happened.

As children, both Laurel and John were encouraged to value and to describe their personal experiences. Although their families didn't share dreams, Laurel and John were free to do so. When Laurel and John created their own family, they continued the tradition of open communication they both valued. However, in their family, dreams have received more direct support as they share their own dreams and encourage their children to do the same. Isabel reports that her friends sometimes find her dreams weird or scary, but she doesn't. Dreams are a natural and intriguing part of her life.

Dream Groups

One of the important ways that we moderns share dreams is in dream groups. Sometimes these groups have leaders, experienced dreamers who have honed their own approach to sharing dreams, and sometimes groups are leaderless. Dream groups in a workshop setting might meet several times during a few days of intensive interaction. Ongoing dream groups can meet weekly, bi-weekly, or monthly. Some dream groups meet for years and become important communities for the group members.

In this era of social media, some dreams groups come together online. The Shift Network of Petaluma, California offers online classes in many transformational disciplines, including dreaming. Part of the structure of their courses on dreaming is a time during each class for participants to call in dreams that the facilitator works with. In addition, a dedicated Facebook page offers a forum for participants to share dreams and comment on one another's dreams. With this kind of platform, people from all over the world are able to work with their dreams together.

In this chapter, we will look at two very different approaches to group dreamwork. The first, and most common approach, offers a supportive setting where the meaning of individual dreams is explored. This approach delves into the meaning of the dream to the dreamer himself and to other group members who will inevitably resonate to the universal issues that emerge in any dream.

These groups provide many kinds of benefits. As group members engage with dreams over time, they observe the meaningful contributions dreams make to life and develop confidence in their own ability to work with dreams effectively. Through exposure to the diverse imagery brought to the group, group members also develop a rich vocabulary of symbols. Finally, and perhaps most importantly, this kind of dream group allows people to connect in authentic, vulnerable ways. As group members share their dreams, their shadow material is inevitably revealed. The group's acceptance of painful parts of the dreamer's personality and life can be healing for the dreamer.

A second approach to group dreamwork presented in this chapter is the co-creation of a composite dream sequence. In this type of group, participants share dreams with the goal of creating a new sequence of dream images from their individual contributions. Participants explore the imagery of their co-created dream, looking for the social, psychological, and spiritual issues in the culture at large.

"If it were my dream . . ."

The late Jeremy Taylor, a Unitarian Universalist minister, led groups that focused on individual dreams. One of the preeminent dream group leaders of the late twentieth and early twenty-first centuries, Taylor led groups in churches, schools, prisons, day treatment centers, residential care centers, and on European study tours.

A foundational principle of Taylor's approach was that every dream image has many personal as well as cultural and cross-cultural connotations. Additionally, every dream has something to say about our current situation, our physical health, and the issues in our collective social experience. Taylor believed that the diverse associations of a group members are uniquely suited to exploring the multiple meanings of any dream.

Taylor's approach was democratic and anti-elitist. He acknowledged that some dream workers are more skilled and more experienced than others, but he also believed that any comment on a dream is shaped by the personality and the unconscious concerns of the commenter. In this sense, even the most skilled psychotherapist offers his own projections.

In his book, *Where People Fly and Water Runs Uphill,* Taylor wrote the following about the inevitable projection involved in working with the dreams of others:

> All efforts to understand dreams more fully are generated out of and through projection, whether undertaken in voluntary groups by amateurs, or one to one in consulting offices by professionals. For this reason, all dream work is ultimately confession. No one has any ideas about the possible meanings in someone else's dream without imaging and enlivening it with his or her own versions of the emotions and images the dreamer reports. For this reason, anything that is said

> about the possible meanings in someone else's dream is always a projection, a reflection of the interior life and symbol dramas of the person making the comment, more than it is a reflection of the possible "objective" significance of the dream itself.[49]

Practically speaking, Taylor's method depended on five words: "If it were my dream." Group members prefaced their insights into one another's dream with these few words that acknowledged the subjectivity of their associations Of course, not every insight or association would be of equal value to the dreamer. In Taylor's groups, dreamers looked for the "aha" flash of recognition (a chill, a jolt of recognition) when something meaningful was offered. Again, there was the democratic movement away from the interpretation of an expert. Each dreamer was the ultimate authority on his own dream.

One of Taylor's most compelling experiences as a group facilitator occurred at San Quentin in the San Francisco Bay Area. For over a year, Taylor ran a drop-in group for inmates at this maximum-security prison. This wasn't an easy task for him. Each time he heard the metal doors lock behind him, he was filled with dread. It was also hard to establish a consistent group of attendees because of outbreaks of violence in the prison, lack of support from administration, and the inmates' ambivalence. To top off a difficult situation, the guards, charged with accompanying the inmates to the group, felt the groups were for "candy asses" and were openly hostile.

One night when Taylor was facilitating this particular group, things promised to be more challenging than usual. Attending the group for the first time was Frank, a huge, volatile man, who was almost seven feet tall and weighed over 300 pounds. As the prisoners approached the chapel where the group was held, Frank lifted other prisoners off the ground, bumped into them, and blocked the doorway to the chapel. The other inmates were clearly wary of this individual who acted like a dangerous, oversized child.

Once the group began, Frank interrupted many times as Taylor explained the approach of the group. Frank made lewd comments as the other attendees tried to share their dreams and then monopolized the group with his own childhood dreams of being attacked by giants. He bragged at how he had repeatedly foiled the giants' attempts to kill him and how these frightening dreams had made him stronger.

Taylor responded to Frank's dreams using the "If it were my dream" format. He mentioned that children experience adults as giants and that childhood dreams about giants may be about the adults in one's life. Taylor then mentioned that dreams of avoiding death are often connected to avoiding a new stage of development and dying to our old ways of being. When Frank heard these things, he became belligerent and got up in Taylor's face. "Wait a minute! You saying I never grew up!" Taylor affirmed that if it were his dream, this would be one meaning of the dream he would consider.

Frank uttered something foul, and withdrew into himself. Taylor felt this was a good sign since Frank was clearly processing something. During Frank's silence, the other men then began to share their own childhood nightmares, particularly dreams of being attacked by giants. When about half the men had shared dreams, Frank pulled out of his reverie and began to blurt out his associations to the dreams of others. Much to everyone's surprise, his associations were insightful and spot on. Others looked at him in shock and then began to share their own associations to the dreams of others. Soon the men were engaged and focused. As Taylor wrote:

> The overall tone of the meeting had changed from negatively tense to something very different—a more positive tension born of focused interest and surprised

> curiosity. Everyone, including the guard, who had by now pulled up a chair and sat down and joined the circle, leaned forward and pulled in closer. The men's voices were getting lower and lower and softer and softer as the dream narratives of being abused and beaten in childhood were shared at greater and greater emotional depth. The stories were depressingly similar, usually involving "corporal punishment" and "discipline" carried out by adult authorities who were often drunk.[50]

In the course of the group, the men abandoned the macho stance that being beaten had made them stronger and began to express their childhood misery. By the end of the group, inmates were listening carefully to Frank's astute, if crudely worded, insights. As the prisoners filed out, Taylor heard several men commenting that they were wrong about Frank, that he was no dummy.

After this powerful evening, Taylor checked in from time to time see if there had been any changes in the inmates. He found out that Frank's behavior became considerably less disruptive and impulsive, and that the inmates treated him differently. There was such a big change that a few months later, Frank was transferred from San Quentin to a medium-security prison.

This story is a powerful example of how dreams can cut below even the most entrenched personas and allow group members to access their common humanity. Sharing childhood dreams about giants allowed these violent men to move away from their tough guy stance and to touch into their shared suffering. "Aha's" happened individually and collectively, and some lasting shifts seemed to have occurred in the participants in the group.

Deep Dreaming

A different approach to group dreamwork moves away from dreams as a resource for personal guidance. This approach focuses on dreams as a reflection of our collective joys and sorrows, and looks for guidance, not just for individuals but for our culture as a whole.

Psychologist Meredith Sabini and longtime dreamworker Richard Russo of The Dream Institute of Northern California have developed a novel process called Deep Dreaming. In this approach to group dreamwork, participants link their individual dreams to form a new sequence of dream images. This sequence is like a larger, composite dream that the group explores to understand the themes and issues of the culture at large.

Each Deep Dreaming session has three separate phases. During the first part, "The Dreaming," participants sit together in a meditative state that connects them to the creativity and mystery of the unconscious. In this phase, participants are invited to share dreams from any time in their lives. As the dream imagery of others washes through participants, their own dreams arise in response. Dreams evoke other dreams and a new sequence of images emerges.

During "The Dreaming," individual dreams are shared in the present tense without any kind of commentary or association. The imagery of many dreams stands side by side, undiluted by interpretation.

In the second part, "Discussion and Exploration," participants return from the meditative state to discuss the images and dreams in the new dream sequence. Just as we associate to images in our individual dreamwork, so in Deep Dreaming participants associate to the imagery of the co-created dream sequence. However, the focus is on understanding cultural issues, rather than the personal meanings of the imagery. For instance, the image of a homeless person might lead to a discussion of homelessness or lack of roots in the cultural at large, rather than in an individual's life.

During "Dream Re-entry," the third and final part of Deep Dreaming, the focus shifts from the cultural perspective to the personal. Participants return to a meditative state to explore a personally meaningful scene in the composite dream sequence. As an example, a participant might chose an image of homelessness that reflects how she feels unrooted or without a home base in her own life. At the conclusion of this phase, participants share the images they have chosen.

Since the beginning of this work in 2004, Sabini and Russo have offered Deep Dreaming to various organizations and to graduate students interested in using this approach. They also have a core group that has met for over ten years. Themes that have emerged include global warming and environmental degradation, homelessness, the suffering of animals, gender issues, and intercultural relations. Strong feminine figures and wisdom from indigenous cultures have appeared as resources in many dreams.

Participants are frequently moved by the compelling imagery that arises in Deep Dreaming sessions. They also report being equally touched by their experience of interconnectedness. As Russo wrote in a recent article:

> During more than a decade of exploring and refining the method, participants repeatedly reported that simply the experience of coming together to dream, and the resultant feelings of interconnectedness, were as important and rewarding as the content of the dreams of any particular session. Typical comments are that it is comforting to know that other people are having dreams similar to their own; that the dreams all seem to be "coming from the same place," and thus they feel close and connected to the other dreamers;

> and that the burden of disturbing dreams seems lessened through understanding that the dreams are not only about personal issues.[51]

My own experience resonates with Russo's comments. Some years ago, I participated in several Deep Dreaming sessions. I particularly remember one that featured many animal dreams. Images of joyfully cavorting with whales and images of a frightening encounter with a bear have stayed with me. I also remember a sad dream about a wounded elephant. Our co-created dream sequence presented many different aspects of our collective relationship to animals. It revealed our shared love of animals as well as our deep grief at how we humans have hurt these wild and beautiful creatures. I came away from this session feeling more connected to animals personally, but also with a more deeply felt understanding of our culture's relationship to animals.

Although the vivid content of this dream sequence has remained with me, I was equally touched, as Russo has suggested, by the intimacy of this process. I was moved by sharing the creativity and mystery of the unconscious with other participants. I was touched by the opportunity to link my unconscious to the unconscious of others and to weave my dream images with theirs. This was a powerful and intimate experience that I've never forgotten.

A Sacred Path

Throughout this book, we've seen how dreams accompany us from early childhood to death, widening our perspective and offering guidance as life unfolds. In this chapter, we have looked at many ways we can share this important part of life with others. Through sharing dreams with family, friends, and compatible dream groups, our personal dreamwork can become part of our development as a culture and as a species.

In the introduction to the book, I shared the dream that first suggested this book to me. In it, a woman received a revelation from God that inspired her to start a church. My dream self was moved by this woman's story and thought that she could collect stories about this kind of revelation. Later, when I worked with this dream, I felt that a revelation from God was an apt metaphor for how dreams function in our life. Soon after, I began gathering dreams for a book about how dreams inspire and guide us.

A few days before completing this book, I encountered another connection between dreaming and church. A participant in Deep Dreaming at the Dream Institute wrote a comment about her experience of Deep Dreaming:

> Deep dreaming holds a place in our community which church used to hold, a place where we can join together in a deep, liminal space to receive through the dreaming, messages from beyond: messages of the ecstatic and messages of the ordinary. When we dream together, we open ourselves to be touched by the Divine. That's why I call it "church."[52]

These two images, connecting dreaming and church, formed bookends for this project. They affirmed that whether we engage with dreams in the privacy of our dream journal or with others, whether we engage with them as individual expressions of our own journey or as a reflection of larger cultural themes, dreamwork is sacred. At a time when the imagery of our religious institutions has lost meaning for many people, our dreams offer fresh, compelling images that expand our understanding and inspire us. As we have seen throughout this book, our dreams meet us at the gateways of life, offering guidance to us as individuals and as a culture.

Explorations

- Are you drawn to sharing your dream life with others?
- In your dream journal, explore how you might benefit from this kind of sharing.
- Of the approaches to sharing dreams in this chapter, which resonate most with you?
- What are the next steps you can take to set the kind of sharing that attracts you?
- If you already share your dreaming with others, what are the significant moments of sharing dreams that you remember?
- How did those moments of sharing dreams contribute to your life and the lives of others?

Acknowledgments

Thanks to my husband, Roger Barry, who always steps up and walks beside me. In addition to being the first set of eyes on all of my writing, he helped with all aspects of publishing and kept my technology humming. Without his unwavering support, this book would never have seen the light of day.

I'm grateful to Wilma Friesema for her ongoing encouragement and her understanding of both dreams and the writing life. Our friendship was born under a bright star.

The writing journey was sweetened by Glori Zeltzer and Laurel Connell, my smart and feisty dream-group women, who supported both my sleeping and my waking dreams.

Lori Kozlowski, my brilliant and intuitive editor, didn't just tell me about the value of this project. She showed me by experimenting with the book's ideas in her own life.

Thanks to friends who have provided support and insight over many years: Marilee Stark, Ellen Denholtz, Claudia Lapp, Barbara McEnerney, Jenny Root, Susan Warner Smith, Denise M. Wallace, Adrienne Amundsen, Elise Morgan, Carole Petiet, and Jerilyn Gilbert. I'm particularly indebted to Lynn Ireland for our years of friendship and for our weekly calls during the writing of this book.

I'm grateful to my sister, Linda Villa, for encouragement, for financial support for this project, and for rallying the troops for my GoFundMe campaign.

And thank you to each and every person who contributed to the GoFundMe campaign that provided so much more than financial support.

Thank you to Dale O'Brien who offered sage advice when it was needed.

A surprise assist came from Ejay Jamb, who generously offered her time and energy to review the chapter on Jane Roberts. Any misunderstanding belongs to me alone.

I'm grateful to Brooke Warner and her talented team, Chris Dumas and Tabitha Lahr, at She Writes Press. Thank you for excellent proofreading and for giving the book the beauty I hoped for.

And last but not least, my deepest thanks to the dreamers who enthusiastically offered their dreams to this project: Dawn Nelson Barankin, Laurel, John, and Isabel Connell, Dale Figtree, Wilma Friesema, David Harris, Glenna Berry Horton, Valerie McCarney, Mimi Nelson Oliver, Carole Petiet, Bob Quinn, Lisanna Rood, Rick Schooley, Prartho Sereno, and Denise M. Wallace. Thanks to the contributors who wish to remain unnamed and to the people who sent dreams that I didn't include in this collection. Every dream I received made a difference.

Notes

1. Annie M. Gordon, "Your Sleep Cycle Revealed," *Psychology Today*, July 26, 2013, http://psychologytoday.com/us/blog/between-you-and-me/201307/your-sleep-cycle-revealed.
2. C. G. Jung, "On the Nature of Dreams," in *Dreams,* trans. R.F.C. Hull (New Jersey: Princeton University Press, 1974), 69.
3. C. G. Jung, *Memories, Dreams, Reflections*, ed. Aniela Jaffé, trans. Richard and Clara Winston (New York: Vintage Books, 1989), Chapter I.
4. Jung, *Memories,* 12.
5. Jung, *Memories,* 14.
6. Jung, *Memories,* Chapter V.
7. Jung, *Memories,* 178.
8. Jung, *Memories,* Chapter VI.
9. Nan Savage Healy, *Toni Wolff & C. G. Jung: A Collaboration* (Los Angeles: Tiberius Press, 2017), Chapter 7.
10. Jung, *Memories,* 180.
11. Jung, *Memories,* 182–183.
12. Jung, *Memories,* 183.
13. Murray Stein, *Jung's Map of the Soul: An Introduction* (Illinois: Carus Publishing Company, 1998). The definition of terms in the following section book was aided by this excellent introduction to Jung's terminology.

14. C. G. Jung, "General Aspects of Dream Psychology, "in *Dreams,* trans. R.F.C, Hull (New Jersey: Princeton University Press, 1974), 31.
15. Sue Watkins, *Speaking of Jane Roberts: Remembering the Author of the Seth Material* (Massachusetts: Moment Point Press, 2001), 12–14, Kindle. edition
16. Jane Roberts, *The Seth Material* (New York: New Awareness Network, Inc., 2001), 10.
17. Roberts, *Seth Material,* 11.
18. Roberts, *Seth Material,* Chapter One.
19. Jane Roberts, *Seth, Dreams and Projections of Consciousness* (New York: New Awareness Inc.,1986), 97.
20. Jane Roberts, *Seth Speaks: The Eternal Validity of the Soul* (California: Amber-Allen Publishing and New World Library, 1994), 70–71.
21. Roberts, *Dreams and Projections,* 220.
22. Roberts, *Seth Material,* Chapter Nineteen.
23. Roberts, *Dreams and Projections,* 316–317
24. Roberts, *Dreams and Projections,* 323.
25. Roberts, *Dreams and Projections,* 325.
26. Roberts, *Dreams and Projections,* 263.
27. Roberts, *Dreams and Projections,* 266.
28. Roberts, *Dreams and Projections,* 268.
29. Roberts, *Dreams and Projections,* 36.
30. Andrew Samuels, Bani Shorter, and Fred Plant, A *Critical Dictionary of Jungian Analysis* (London: Routledge & Kegan Paul, Ltd., 1986), 122.
31. Kate Marcus, "Childhood Dreams and Experiences: Intimations of the Future," *Psychological Perspectives,* 48 (2005): 261.
32. Kelly Bulkeley et al., "Earliest Remembered Dreams," in*Dreaming* 15:3(2005): ,210.
33. Prartho Sereno, *Indian Rope Trick* (San Francisco: Blue Light Press, 2018), 73.

34. Rumi, *The Illuminated Rumi,* trans. Coleman Barks (New York: Broadway Books, 1997), 49.
35. Jung, *Dreams,* 76.
36. Jung, *Memories*, 85.
37. Kathleen Sullivan, *Recurring Dreams: A Journey to Wholeness* (California: The Crossing Press, 1998), 4.
38. Jung, *Dreams,* 79.
39. Edward G. Whitmont and Sylvia Perrera, *Dreams: A Portal to the Source* (London and New York: Routledge, 1989), 119.
40. Montague Ullman and Nan Zimmerman, *Working with Dreams: Self-Understanding, Problem-Solving and Enriched Creativity Through Dream Appreciation* (Los Angeles: Jeremy P. Tarcher, 1979), 26.
41. Rumi, *Illuminated*, 77.
42. Edward Tick, *The Practice of Dream Healing* (Illinois: Quest Books, 2001), Chapters One–Seven.
43. Homer, *Homeric Hymns,* trans. Andrew Lang, ISBN 13:978-1522721215, 2015, 62.
44. John Sanford, *Dreams*: *God's Forgotten Language* (New York: Harper One, 1968), 42.
45. Sanford, *Dreams*. 42–43.
46. Hafiz, "It Felt Love" in *The Gift,* trans. Daniel Ladinsky (New York: The Penguin Group, 1999), 121.
47. Stanley Krippner, Fariba Bogzaran, and André Percia De Carvalho, *Extraordinary Dreams and How to Work with Them* (New York: State University of New York Press, 2002), 148–149.
48. Gn 28:11-22. KJV.
49. Jeremy Taylor, Where *People Fly and Water Runs Uphill: Using Dreams to Tap the Wisdom of the Unconscious* (New York: Warner Books, 1992), 135.
50. Taylor, *People Fly*, 148.

51. Richard Russo, "Culture Dreaming (or Deep Dreaming)," in *Dreams: Understanding Biology, Psychology, and Culture,* eds. Robert J. Hoss, Katja Valli, and Robert P. Gongloff (California: Greenwood, 2019), 545.
52. "Culture-Dreaming," The Dream Institute of Northern California, accessed July 20, 2019, https://dream-institute.org/culture-dreaming.

References

Bulkeley, Kelly and Patricia M. Bulkley. *Children's Dreams*. Maryland: Rowman & Littlefield Publishers, Inc., 2012.

Bulkeley, Kelly and Patricia Bulkley. *Dreaming Beyond Death: A Guide to Pre-Death Dreams and Visions*. Boston: Beacon Press, 2005.

Bulkeley, Kelly, Bitsy Broughton, Anita Sanchez, and Joanne Stiller. "Earliest Remembered Dreams." *Dreaming* 15:3 (2005): 205–222.

Bryant, Dorothy. *The Kin of Ata Are Waiting for You*. New York: Random House and Berkeley: Moon Books, 1971.

Domhoff, G. William. *The Mystique of Dreams*. Berkeley and Los Angeles: University of California Press, 1985.

The Dream Institute of Northern California. "Culture Dreaming." Accessed July 20, 2019. http://dream-isntitute.org/culture-dreaming.

Epel, Naomi. *Writers Dreaming: Twenty-six Writers Talk about Their Dreams and the Creative Process*. New York: Vintage Books, 1991.

Freud, Sigmund. *The Interpretation of Dreams*. Edited and translated by James Strachey. New York: Basic Books, 1955.

Gordon, Amie M. "Your Sleep Cycle Revealed." *Psychology Today*. July 26, 2013. Accessed January 15, 2019. http://psychologytoday.com/us/blog/between-you-and-me/201307/your-sleep-cycle-revealed.

Hafiz. *The Gift*. Translated by Daniel Ladinsky. New York: Putnam Penguin, 1999.

Healy, Nan Savage. *Toni Wolff & C. G. Jung: A Collaboration*. Los Angeles: Tiberius Press, 2017.

Hillman, James. *The Dream and the Underworld*. New York: Harper Perennial, 1979.

Homer. *Homeric Hymns*, trans. Andrew Lang. ISBN: 13:978-1522721215, 2015.

Jung, C.G. *Memories, Dreams, Reflections*. Edited by Aniela Jaffé, translated by. Richard and Clara Winston. New York: Vintage Books, 1989.

———. *Dreams, from The Collected Works of C.G. Jung, Volumes 4, 8, 12, 16*. Translated by R.F. C. Hull. New Jersey: Princeton University Press, Bollingen Series XX, 1974.

———. *The Red Book*. Edited by Sonu Shamdasani. New York: W.W. Norton & Co., 2009.

Krippner, Stanley, Fariba Bogzaran, and André Percia De Carvalho. *Extraordinary Dreams and How to Work with Them*. New York: State University of New York Press, 2002.

Lawrence, W. Gordon. *Introduction to Social Dreaming*. London: Karnac, 2005.

Marcus, Kate. "Childhood Dreams and Experiences: Intimations of the Future." *Psychological Perspectives* 48 (2005): 261–273.

Oliver, Mary. *Dream Work*. New York: Atlantic Monthly Press, 1986.

Roberts, Jane. *Seth, Dreams and Projections of Consciousness*. New York: New Awareness Network Inc., 1998.

———. *Seth Speaks: The Eternal Validity of the Soul*. California: Amber-Allen Publishing and New World Library. 1994.

———. *The Seth Material*. New York: New Awareness Network Inc., 1970.

Rumi. *The Illuminated Rumi*. Translated by Coleman Barks, illustrated by Michael Green. New York: Broadway Books, 1997.

Russo, Richard. "Culture Dreaming (or Deep Dreaming)." In *Dreams: Understanding Biology, Psychology, and Culture*, edited by Robert J. Hoss, Katja Valli, and Robert P. Gongloff, 534-548. California: Greenwood, 2019.

Samuels, Andrew, Bani Shorter, and Fred Plant. *A Critical Dictionary of Jungian Analysis* London: Routledge & Kegan Paul, Ltd, 1986.

Sanford, John. *Dreams: God's Forgotten Language.* New York: Harper One, 1968.

Sereno, Prartho. *Indian Rope Trick.* San Francisco: Blue Light Press, 2018.

Stein, Murray. *Jung's Map of the Soul: An Introduction.* Illinois: Carus Publishing Company, 1998.

Sullivan, Kathleen. *Recurring Dreams: A Journey to Wholeness.* California: The Crossing Press, 1998.

Taylor, Jeremy. *Where People Fly and Water Runs Uphill: Using Dreams to Tap the Wisdom of the Unconscious.* New York: Warner Books, 1992.

Tick, Edward. *The Practice of Dream Healing.* Illinois: Quest Books, 2001.

Ullman, Montague and Nan Zimmerman. *Working with Dreams: Self-Understanding, Problem-Solving, and Enriched Creativity Through Dream Appreciation.* Los Angeles: Jeremy P. Tarcher Inc., 1979.

Von Franz, Marie-Louise. *Dreams.* Boston and London: Shambhala, 1998.

——. *On Dreams and Death.* Boston: Shambhala, 1987.

Watkins, Sue. *Speaking of Jane Roberts: Remembering the Author of the Seth Material.* Massachusetts: Moment Point Press, 2001. Kindle.

Whitmont, Edward G. & Sylvia Brinton Perera. *Dreams, A Portal to the Source.* London and New York: Routledge, 1989.

About the Author

Kathryn Ridall, PhD, has worked as a psychotherapist in the San Francisco Bay Area and on the Central Coast of California for thirty years. She was a university instructor as well as a clinical supervisor in the Department of Transpersonal Psychology at the Bay Area's John F. Kennedy University. She is the author of the bestselling *Channeling: How to Reach Out to Your Spirit Guides* (Bantam, 1988) as well as of three poetry chapbooks and two poetry anthologies that she edited. She has been following her own dreams since she was three years old and has followed the dreams of her clients throughout her many years of clinical practice.

Made in United States
Troutdale, OR
12/15/2023